The Well of
From Faery Healing to

R.J. Stewart is a Scot, an author and a composer. He now lives in the United States where he was formally admitted as a "resident alien of extra-ordinary ability," a category awarded only to those of exceptional and formally recognized achievements in the arts or sciences.

His books have been published in many languages, and he is widely acknowledged as an authority on mythology, legends, magical arts, and ancient traditions. As a composer, R.J. Stewart has written and recorded music for feature films, television, and theater production, working with directors such as Tony Richardson, Jim Henson. He has also worked on a number of award winning BBC films. His best selling books include *The Merlin Tarot, Celtic Gods Celtic Goddesses, The UnderWorld Initiation,* and *The Miracle Tree: Demystifying Qabalah.*

For a full list of books and recordings see www.rjstewart.net.

SELECTED TITLES BY THE SAME AUTHOR

*Earlier books by R.J. Stewart in the UnderWorld and
Faery series, and recording are referred to in various chapters:*

1. *The UnderWorld Initiation* (1985 UK and later US editions)
2. *Earth Light* (1991 UK and later US editions)
3. *Power Within the Land* (1992 UK and later US editions)
4. *The Living World of Faery* (1995 UK and later US editions)

Also:

5. *The Miracle Tree: Demystifying Qabalah.* 2003, New Page Books, NJ, USA

6. *The Secret Commonwealth of Elves, Fauns and Fairies* (1692) Rev. Robert Kirk. New edition with commentary by R.J. Stewart, originally published by Element Books UK, now available as free online book at www.dreampower.com.

Recordings

7. *Ballad Magic*: a live CD of a presentation and concert, in which magical ballads are explored, and sung in the authentic traditional style, with an audience.

8 *More Magical Songs:* Cassette or CD of original magical songs by R.J. Stewart.

If you cannot obtain these books or recordings in your local book store, you will find all of the above, plus many more, at www.rjstewart.net where can purchase them online.

The Well of Light:

From Faery Healing
to Earth Healing

*The Mystery
of the Double Rose*

R.J. Stewart

R.J. Stewart
Books

Cover art by Andrew Goldys.
Internal line drawings by Martin Bridge
from designs by R.J. Stewart.

Printed in the USA
Reprinted © 2006

A catalog record for this book is
available from the Library of Congess

ISBN: 978-0-9791402-1-1

R.J. Stewart
Books
PO Box 802
Arcata, CA 95518
www.rjstewart.net

Contents

PREFACE TO THE WELL OF LIGHT

For the last ten years or so, I have been leading workshops on Faery Healing. These classes began as historical and folkloric explorations based on old traditional material from Scotland, Ireland, and Europe. They were taught at various locations in the United States and Britain, and gradually developed and expanded into the material found in this book. The original idea was to talk about the old methods, preserved for centuries among country people, which included laying on of hands, working with stones and plants, and healing humans and animals. Simple healing arts are always found in association with the faery tradition in one form or another. As in all of my workshops and classes, there was an emphasis on practical experience – on the spiritual and subtle energetic aspects of the subject, in this case, Faery Healing.

After the first couple of workshops, things started to happen, and the theme began to take a subtle impetus and direction of its own. Whenever the group did a meditation or vision, some people would begin to feel subtle energies working through their bodies, especially into the hands. I began to sense some very specific faery contacts which would always appear when we worked with the healing material. What was happening? It soon became clear that we were tapping into a living tradition, still active, with spirit beings ready to respond and work with us. This did not come out of nothing, I should add, for most of the groups that I taught had already been working with intentional contact with faery beings. They worked with methods that we had experienced together in previous series of workshops, or from those described in my books on the Faery and UnderWorld traditions. The foundation had been laid before, but the nature of the faery edifice that rose up was surprising and powerful.

This book and CD represent the core of the material taught in my workshops, along with some additional new material never before published or taught, especially the section on *The Mystery of the Double Rose*. This new material will be included in my ongoing work with small groups for the future.

I encourage you try this spiritual path for yourself. It is highly transformative and deeply rewarding. It will change your life, and, as we must ultimately hope and strive for, it will contribute to healing changes in our world.

This foreword ends with a prayer and invocation that I have used in Faery Healing for some years. Take it out into the world with you and use it freely.

With us is the Grace of the Shining Ones in the Mystery of Earth Light.
Peace to all Signs and Shadows, Radiant Light to all Ways of Darkness,
and the Living One of Light, Secret Unknown, Forever.

You can find out more about workshops and classes by going to www.dreampower.com and about books and recordings at www.rjstewart.net.

R.J. Stewart, 2003

ACKNOWLEDGEMENTS

I would like to thank the many students and fellow workers in Faery and UnderWorld spirituality who have worked with me over the years, especially those who have taken part in the many Faery Healing classes and workshops in the United States from 1993 to the present day. Their support, their experiences, and their questions have contributed towards my writing of this book, especially in my working out of techniques to publish for general use, now and in the future.

Also, Jenny Stracke for her work on the copy editing and formatting of the book.

Cover, CD artwork, and line drawings, by Martin Bridge from designs by R.J. Stewart © 2004, visit www.martin.ritualarts.org.

Some parts of this book have previously appeared on the Dreampower website, www.dreampower.com and in earlier articles on the Faery tradition and UnderWorld.

And, I must also thank and acknowledge those invisible Allies, Cousins, and Co-Walkers, Companion Creatures, Go-Betweens, and Mentors of the spiritual realm of our Earth, which is the Faery Realm and UnderWorld that forms the subject and source of this book.

R.J. Stewart
California, Winter 2003

Introduction

The Well of Light: From Faery Healing to Earth Healing is part of an ongoing series of books which I have written from experience, both my own and that of my students and fellow workers, based on practical research and intentional team-work to open out our understanding of those powerful realms of consciousness and being, embodied in Faery tales, myths, legends, folk magic, and the literature of the ancient world. Earlier books in this series can be found in the Bibliography, and are occasionally cited or quoted herein. You will benefit enormously from reading and working with these earlier books that laid the foundation for *The Well of Light*, but you do not have to read or study them to undertake the methods that are taught herein. This book stands alone, and offers many techniques and insights into Faery Healing that have never been published, and are unknown in most contemporary texts on Faery magic.

THE METHODS ARE FROM BOTH
DIRECT EXPERIENCE AND TRADITION...

The Well of Light: From Faery Healing to Earth Healing is the result of more than 30 years of work in the Faery and UnderWorld magical and spiritual traditions, and the last ten or more years of practical work in Faery Healing itself, both teaching and learning with groups of people in many different places. The nature of these Faery and UnderWorld traditions today, which is somewhat different from their folkloric and ancient sources, is discussed in depth in the following chapters. Included are many practical examples that will bring the reader into a better relationship, and a more full experience, of what may be found within the greater and radiant consciousness that such traditions embody. In this introduction, I will summarize and describe the main aspects of the book, and therefore, the way in which it was written.

Faery Healing is a form of spiritual healing known in folkloric tradition. It implies a working relationship between humans and the spiritual forces of the land or region in which they live. The healer works closely with Faery (spirit) allies in Faery Healing: they can do things that we cannot, and we can do things that they cannot. Many remarkable results are possible through working together! It has long been reported that specific healing skills were practiced in the folkloric Faery Traditions of Britain, Ireland, and Europe. In this book we begin with the folkloric foundation, but extend many of the ideas and techniques into new areas, previously unknown and never before published. Faery Healing becomes, for the modern era, Earth Healing, a way of healing the wounded relationship between humanity and the planet.

Faery Healing is about living consciousness, and our relationship and participation within such living consciousness. Though there are occasional references to folklore and traditional sources, and early texts in the chapters that follow, this is not a book exclusively on folklore or Faery customs; there are many books that deal with the folkloric material in ways ranging from highly academic studies to banal, even insulting, nonsense. This, however, is a *textbook for practical experience of Faery Healing and Earth Healing* written within the living spiritual traditions of the Faery realm and UnderWorld. This is a book that helps you, the reader, to experience substantially altered consciousness, and to enter into, and return out of, this altered consciousness at will.

Make no mistake, the Faery Tradition, Faery Healing, and the related UnderWorld magical arts are not quaint practices of by-gone days, but *modes of consciousness*. Our participation within these arts can bring about very strong and defined changes of consciousness and subtle energy through specific practices. These practices are enshrined, albeit in a fragmentary and cloaked manner, in those older ancestral traditions handed down through story, song and custom. In a book of this sort we go further than merely restating the folkloric content of Faery Healing or Faery magic (something which is adequately provided by a number of sources that the reader can easily find with an internet search, in addition to the Bibliography offered at the end of this book). We go further because we seek to apply the foundational material, the magical wisdom of our ancestors, and bring it alive in modern practice. It becomes something that we *do*, rather than something that we *read about*.

Inner Contact From Faery Consciousness...

So far I have outlined only two aspects of this book: ancestral folk-loric tradition, and a contemporary restatement of such tradition to create practical methods for modern readers. There is a third aspect, which is crucial not merely to this book, but to all under-standing and practice of spiritual magic, and in this case, to the practice of Faery Healing. This aspect is the *inner contact*, the living consciousness and participation that gives rise to many of the teachings and practices herein. The deepest material in this book comes from years of working with inner contacts. This is particularly true for *The Mystery of the Double Rose*, which arises from themes that I have explored in several earlier books, but here are opened out for the first time, at a deeper level revealing their true inner content and magical potential.

By "inner contact" I mean actual communion and contact with Faery allies, with those spiritual beings that are our closest cousins in the metaphysical realms, in the natural realms, and in the mysterious places-in-between. I have included some items from direct inner contact in several chapters, and have discussed how inner contact works, and how I have translated the contact teachings into words for our use within the book.

Once you start working Faery magic, you soon discover that it is teamwork. Of course it is – what would be the point otherwise? It is not symbolism or fantasy, but practical teamwork shared between humans and spiritual allies. If this idea makes you uncomfortable, you have not yet shed the smothering and sour old garment of post-Christian conditioning, and this book is probably not for you.

If, however, you are open to the idea that the world is very different from the consensual propaganda taught in schools and reinforced by television, then I am sure that you will find much to inspire and intrigue you in this book. I can assert this because writing it has inspired and intrigued me – not, of course, the long and patient assembly of text and references and checking grammar that is the dedicated labor of any competent author, but the discovery of new material. This new material comes from Inner Contacts: I commune with my allies, my Faery allies, and so come into specific teachings and practices. Some of these are found in this book. The writing, the exposition, the words are mine, but the inner concepts and the core methods come from Faery consciousness.

HEALING A WOUNDED WORLD...

If we are to truly work within a healing tradition that will transform our outer world, we must also work very hard to form good connections with the consciousness of other living beings on Earth. This is not achieved through romanticism on weekend breaks in the woods, on safaris, or on tour ships that pollute the Antarctic. It comes only through steady unceasing patient work to relate to our allies, cousins, and co-walkers of the Faery and creature realms. My initial task as writer and mediator is to attune, commune, describe, and offer the resulting teachings, but *our* task, all of us together, is to put them into daily practice. Such an ongoing and dedicated practice in the heart of the concrete and plastic city is inestimably more valuable than an occasional trip to the country. It is the practice that is important, not just the location. For, if it is done well and done deeply, the practice transforms both the location and ourselves.

So a large proportion of the material in this book comes direct from the living consciousness of the Faery Tradition, though the writing out of this into human text is my own, as are any faults therein. When you work with the practical methods described in the following chapters, they will put you into deeper contact with the Faery realm and with the arts of Faery Healing.

THE THREEFOLD STAGES OF FAERY HEALING...

Throughout this book, I have emphasized that Faery Healing is not about a human focused need-based healing, such as we are accustomed to expect, and pay for, in modernist culture. There are several stages to Faery Healing, and we usually experience them in the following order:

1. Faery Healing is first and foremost about transformation through interaction with other orders of life, the Faery races, the living creatures of the land and sea, and the plants. This transformation is, of itself, a healing experience.

2. The next stage is mediation of the subtle forces, the life and death forces, in alliance with our cousins, allies, and co-walkers of the Faery realm. This is the stage that includes, but is by no means limited to, direct healing through the Seven Aptitudes (which are described in Chapter 3). Here the healing forces may flow to humans, animals, places, or in a more general way (and just as needful and significant) they may flow unconditionally out into the wounded world.

3. The third stage is Earth Healing, which has within it three further stages. Earth Healing is where we come away from the focused

needs or imbalances of an individual entity, be it human or other, and work on larger tasks. This is always team-work, wherein humans and Faery allies work together. It cannot be done by humans alone, or indeed, by the Faery races alone. One of the aims of this book is to promote understanding of one of the core teachings of the Faery Tradition: *there are things that They can do that We cannot, and there are things that We can do that They cannot.* In Faery Healing, as in all Faery magic, both sides, human and Faery, work according to this primary law, and thus seek to work together in harmony and mutual respect. There is no idea, anywhere in this book, that faeries are imaginary constructs, psychological archetypes (in the Jungian sense), "thought forms" or "helpers." They are real, independent, living beings with which we share the world, the sacred Planet Earth.

The three stages of Earth Healing are as follows:

3.1   Undertaking larger tasks, which are often about the vitality of land or sea, is the first stage. This may involve team-work on cleansing and healing locations that have been polluted or damaged, and on opening out the spiritual forces in "dead" zones created by human development. This first level may also include working on species of creatures that have been impacted by human pollution or abuse. There is a further aspect of this work, which is similar to inoculation, immunization, and defense.

3.2   The second level is carried out deeper down, in the UnderWorld itself. It consists of healing subtle rifts and imbalances that are, both metaphysically and literally, in the realms beneath. At this level, we work not on visible and tangible surface tasks or imbalances, or upon living beings of the outer world. Instead we work remotely, in deep team consciousness, upon the subtle forces of the land and sea. These are usually presented to us in a visionary form. A classic example of this type of work is found in the section on *Bridge Making* (in Chapter 6). A further level of this second stage involves conscious cooperation in the emergence of new life forms from the deep Dream of the World, mediated by the Shining Ones in the core and heart of Earth Light.

3.3   The third level is deep in the living consciousness and energy of the planet, and is done in that place where the Earth Light and the Shining Ones originate. This is mostly in the manner of formless, wordless Communion. The very act of building such a communion is, in itself, the Earth Healing. This third level, or mode, is only accessible after training and practice in the first two, though we may touch upon it in visionary experiences. To help us grasp this level, I have included a vision that I use with my more experienced students and groups, called the *Sacred Mountain* (in Chapter 6).

Now that I have introduced the book, I would invite and encourage you to read next the short section on *How to Use This Book,* before you jump into the practical work of Faery Healing or listen to the CD that comes with this book. For this type of publication, I have found such "how to" sections to be invaluable, both for my own works (whereby they help me to clarify how the reader might use the book as I write it, and thus improve the communication between us all!), and in those books by other writers, whose work I read, and from which I learn.

How to Use This Book

- First, listen all the way through to the CD.
- Second, read the book through like a novel.
- Third, do the exercises in the first chapter, without fail.
- Fourth, work with the book chapter by chapter.
- But before you do any of this, please take a few minutes to read on …

There are several levels to this book, for in the Faery realm it is possible to say many things at once. As author, part of my task has been to separate out these simultaneous, and sometimes paradoxical, statements, methods, and insights. There are many ways to work with a book of this sort, but as always, I recommend that you read it straight through, like a novel, before trying any practical work. For most of us this is difficult, as we long to jump in and do things, but your patience will be well rewarded. Why so? Because as you read right through the book, you will be storing in your mind many things, thoughts, images, and concepts, some of which may not make sense on a first reading, plus (I trust) even more things that do indeed make sense, inspire, inform, and create realizations! If you are so inclined, you could make some notes from your first reading, though there is no need to do so, as this is not an academic text but an inspirational one.

The more you can seat Faery and UnderWorld work in living memory, the better it will function for you. You cannot take your notebook (paper or electronic) to the Faery realm, or into the spirit world at large. Bill Gates notwithstanding.

Once the text has been read, you will find that the early meditations and visionary exercises in the first chapter, entitled *Essential Definitions*, will begin to relate strongly to your reading, and interact with your memory of the text, perhaps on an unconscious level at first, but soon emerging into that new consciousness where the human and Faery realms meet. This is the threshold place where fresh things come, inspired, into the consciousness. For a psychologist, these "fresh things" are a result of processes of cognition or appearances from the unconscious mind. This may indeed be so, but they also come from inner contacts, a theme that is central to this book, and to the Faery Tradition itself.

So, having listened to the CD, and read the book through, please begin your practical work with the first chapter, *Essential Definitions*. This is a set of short essays on basics such as the nature of the Faery Realm, Elementals, Titans and Giants, Time and Ancestors, along with a set of simple *forms* or exercises for opening out consciousness. I have used the word *forms* because these exercises are not text-based visualizations, though we access them, of course, through the text. Another term that might be helpful is *empowered visions*. These simple forms, and the later more complex forms, are empowered by inner contact and by subtle forces. They are not merely constructs written to arouse a sensation or a mood. When you do them, something happens: that something comes from the subtle forces and the attuned inner contacts that you reach through the form, through the working.

I would recommend that you do each of the forms in *Essential Definitions* once you have read their relevant sections. You should do them at least three times each, in your own time, at your own pace. They only take a few minutes each, though you can spend as much time as you wish in the communion phase of any of the visions. You can then continue to do them whenever and wherever you wish, as they are simple, direct and easy to learn. They will substantially prepare the way for your deeper work with Faery Healing and Earth Healing.

Some Guidelines for Using The Exercises

Perhaps you have not done this kind of thing before, but through-out the main text I assume that many readers have worked with inner vision, and are experienced in some kind of inner work, as this is not a total beginner's book. Even if you are experienced, you should consider the following method which offers some insights into how inner working actually functions for us as contemporary people. There are four stages, all of which mutually interact, and are not truly separated from one another:

1. The text stage, reading and assimilating (reading silently, then aloud)
2. The visual stage, intentionally building images (using the imagi-nation in a focused manner without distraction or meandering)
3. The feeling stage, experiencing the inner contact and *feeling* the subtle forces. (Not merely emotional impetus or personal feelings, but a sense of touch or body memory. For example, think of how a place you have visited on your travels *feels*. This inner touch and memory is what will carry you to and fro to inner places such as the Crossroads, the Well of Light, and the UnderWorld.
4. The total memory stage: with practice, you will find that you can remember the *totality* of the working, and reproduce its effects *backwards* from the feeling/body memory of the third stage. This is actually an easy process that occurs rapidly, though it seems complex to describe or read about. It is easy because we all have an inherent ability to do this … no matter how out of practice we have become due to the artificial constraints of modernist life.

So, experienced or not, here is the basic method, which, if you are working from text, is to begin by reading the form/exercise through to yourself *aloud*:
1. Read it aloud a few times until you are familiar with it. Some people like to tape themselves reading it, as this helps to seat it in the memory. Taping works well for the basic short forms, but may be a chore for the longer ones.

2. When you are fairly comfortable and familiar with the contents, work inwardly through the form – i.e. do it. Keep the book with you, but try not to refer to it. Go for the stages of the empowered vision, step by step, rather than the sentences of text describing it. Only refer to the book if you forget one of the steps. Try to use the text as a clue, not as dogma. Aim for the visionary stages. If you do not have a strong visual imagination, do not concern yourself or think of this as a barrier; there is far too much emphasis on the visual in our culture. The most advanced spiritual work goes far beyond vision into active communion. Merely think, feel, and see your way through the stages of each form. It will come alive for you.

3. You will know when it comes alive, because you will feel subtle sensations, often in the body rather than through visionary experiences. Sometimes you will, indeed, see the Faery beings, but more often you feel their presence and your body will respond to their subtle forces. Learn to trust this sensory experience.

4. With some practice, you will simply remember the *form*. Go for the totality of it, remember the feeling, and you are there. Now the real magic begins.

USING THE CD

This book comes with a CD of empowered visions, with music on the flute and 80 stringed psaltery. Most people will want to listen to the CD immediately: I know that I always do when I buy a CD! As with the book, listen to the recording all the way through. Just absorb it: you may go deeply into the visionary forms, or you may simply listen. Let it work for you spontaneously at first. The content of the CD is, in fact, part of a progression which you will find in the suggested work program at the end of the book. You do not have to follow the work program, but I can assure you that it will be helpful in your development of skills in both Faery Healing and in UnderWorld and Faery magic in general. The choice is yours. It is more helpful and effective to find a small number of forms or workings and do them frequently with dedication, than to slog through any work program or text step by step without relating to it. Take it easy, there is no rush or panic. Indeed, you will find that your body and inner sense will respond rapidly enough to the material, both on the CD, and in the book. We already have innate aptitudes for Faery Healing, and we already have experience of the spiritual worlds, albeit cloaked from us by the drudgery and tedium of the modernist world. The poetry and music on the CD helps to whip that cloak aside.

Once you have worked with the CD a number of times, you will easily remember the forms or empowered visions on it. They include some powerful formulaic invocations, which you will be able to repeat inwardly and work with anywhere, any time.

The work program also shows how to integrate the tracks on the CD into the material of the main text, step by step.

Working Through The Book

Having listened to the CD, having read the book through like a novel, and then having worked with the simple forms in the first chapter of *Essential Definitions,* you will be ready to work through the remaining chapters of the book one by one. As always, I would recommend that you step through each stage in the order they appear, chapter by chapter. Do each form at least once, but then move on to the next, until you have done them all at least once. Use the work program at the end of the book if you wish, but do not fail to do each form, in order, at least once. This simple method is intense, and will greatly open out your inner senses and aptitudes. Do not get stuck on any one stage, for if it does not work for you now, it will work later. And besides, it may be working at a deep level, to surface later through some as yet unknown pattern in your spiritual life. This is Faery magic, and it does not work like installing software.

Intense concentration and repeated effort on any one item are usually counterproductive. It is better to have experienced the whole sequence than to merely focus on one part of it. If you are unsure about the "results" of any stage, simply move on to the next. Do not place value judgments or merit awards on your inner experiences; they are not college studies or employment roles. Let us be thankful!

As with all skills, the whole is more than the sum of the parts. There are what seem to be graded exercises in this book, from the shortest and simplest to the more complex. There are stages of interaction, from the short visit to the UnderWorld, to highly empowered exchanges of energy through meditation of Allies, Go-Betweens, and the Great Ones of the tradition. Yet the simplest form is also the most powerful, and the so-called "beginner" forms are those that you will use again at the deepest level when you have gained much experience in your relationships with the Faery realm and UnderWorld.

Once you have worked through it all, take a break for a while, and let things settle within you and mature. At some later time, read through the entire book again, like a novel. You will be surprised at how different it seems, and how much hidden material leaps out at you once you have experienced the inner contact and practiced Faery Healing. This occurs because the Faery and UnderWorld consciousness has many simultaneous levels, whereas plain text does not.

Finally, I will say what I always say in workshops and classes: do not expect or demand of yourself to remember everything. Some things will stand out strongly and vividly, others will be vague or even difficult.

The way to use this book, as described above, will polarize and clarify many things for you, especially your spiritual sensitivity and your Aptitudes for Faery Healing. After that? Just do it – it is your gift, your right, your responsibility, your joy, and your true role in the world.

R.J. Stewart, 2003

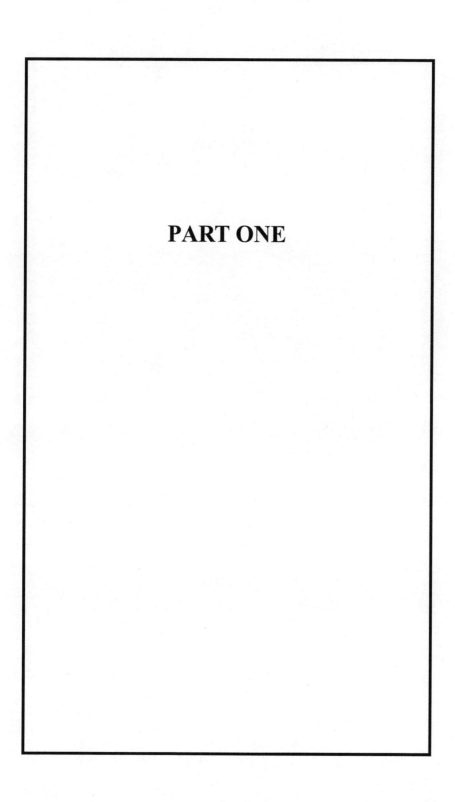

PART ONE

1. Essential Definitions

In this Chapter you will find a series of short essays that define the essentials of the Faery Tradition, the UnderWorld, Titans and Giants, Time and Consciousness, and other related subjects. They were written over a period of time to answer many of the basic questions that people ask in workshops and classes, so they arise from the thoughts and needs of students, Faery enthusiasts, and practicing magicians of many schools of thought and practice. These essays are intended as simple definitions and introductions to many of the ideas in this book, and they describe many of the core concepts that are explored in more detail throughout the book. It is recommended that you read this chapter first, before proceeding to the in-depth material in the main text.

FAERIES, NATURE SPIRITS AND ELEMENTALS

During my travels in the United States teaching workshops, one question keeps recurring in various forms: "What is the difference (and/or the connection) between Faeries, Nature Spirits, and Elementals?"

Like most questions, there are several possible answers, and none of them are completely true. However, we can draw near to the truth of the matter, especially through meditation, vision, and direct experience of the spirit world of our planet. I do not refer to the spirit world of angels, but to that of our planet, which teems with spiritual life. In the Faery and UnderWorld traditions, we are concerned with the living planet and its spiritual dimensions, not with a remote spirituality of so-called "higher planes." We repudiate and scorn the pernicious notion that the Earth is somehow sinful, and that the Earthly realm, and the Lunar realm that enfolds it, must be somehow rejected in order to reach spiritual enlightenment. Enlightenment begins at home, and Earth is our home. Later, when we have experienced the transformative power of the Earth Light, we discover that the Earth and Moon have their home within the consciousness of Sun and Planets, and that the solar world has its home in the Stars. By being at home on Earth, therefore, we are discovering that we are already at home in the Sun and Stars.

So this essay on Faeries, Nature Spirits, and Elementals is intended to help set the scene for your own experience, to offer some simple thoughts, ideas, questions, and challenges. These challenges apply especially to popular established dogma and propaganda about Faeries, Nature Spirits, and Elementals. As with most spiritual matters, let us begin at the end of the list, and work our way towards the beginning.

Elementals

Some years ago I had a conversation with the author Isaac Bonewitz. He said (approximately) that Elementals only exist in the formal temple or lodge where the ritual magician has created them. We discussed this for some time, and I think we disagreed in a friendly manner. However, his statement made me think about the popular idea of Elementals as it is presented in modern literature on magic, paganism, witchcraft, earth mysteries, and so forth. There certainly is, I concluded, a problem with the way Elementals are often described, which is that they are components of pure Air, Fire, Water, or Earth, with a basic consciousness inherent in their own nature, but nothing else.

If we think about Elementals as small components of "pure" Air,

Fire, Water, and Earth with some sort of limited consciousness, we are making them too abstract and too small. These "pure" Elementals are what Isaac Bonewitz was talking about, and they are indeed mainly found where they have been impressed into existence by temple magic. They have no independent existence in nature, and will fade if they are not constantly maintained. This is similar to many experimental or analytical situations in science, which cannot be maintained outside laboratory conditions. The magical temple is the laboratory of the magician, of course, but we need to relate to the living world rather than create isolated entities that have no life beyond the magical field of their creation.

During the late 1970s, I was at sea in the English Channel traveling through a terrible storm in which several ships, including sailboats in the Fastnet Race, were lost. This experience left me in no doubt about the existence and nature of Elementals: they are large conglomerate beings of one primary Element, but with the other three also present. Thus the Storm lived as many huge wind Elementals (Air) and the mountainous seas (Water). It was also itself, a Storm. This made it, for the duration of its life, a Nature Spirit, defined by both power and place. Its power was of the many Elementals of Air and Water, and its place was the English Channel, where it lived and moved.

Elementals are perceived and encountered during a gathering of forces into undeniable, visible, tangible patterns: the forest fire, the volcanic eruption, the tornado, the earthquake. Anyone with spiritual sensitivity who has been in any such events will confirm the presence of a host of beings that, like a hive or complex organism, make up the greater being – the total.

This is not unusual for us to comprehend, of course. The human body is exactly such a compound organism. Billions of living creatures work together to create that same body that we use to slump on the couch and watch television, or to walk around the world and commune with the Faery allies, trees, plants, and living creatures. The choice is ours: the body is not.

Thus, to attempt to isolate "an Elemental" is like isolating an atom – perhaps exactly the same. It is a technical or artificial process.

They all exist in Nature, but do not exist naturally in isolation, for they are defined utterly by one another. Many Fire Elementals make a bonfire, or a firestorm, but they can do so only through interaction with those of Air and Earth to build that larger Elemental being. It is a matter of relativity and not one of abstract absolutes.

We are already Elementals!

Do not forget, ever, that you are already Elementals. There is not one, but several of them, most likely a large complex number, within yourself. Our bodies are made of Water, Earth, Fire, and Air. Our consciousness and energies are Elemental. That is, the philosophical or metaphysical concept of the Four Elements as relative states of motion and energy, but not limited to the modern idea of elements as defined in chemistry and physics. So, to find Elementals, we need look no further than our own bodies and moods. And, I propose, we should pay much more attention to the way our bodies and emotions interact with places and with weather changes. In the Faery-based spiritual traditions, interaction with weather and with place brings deep insights. This idea of ourselves as Elementals raises a fundamental theme for our discussion, and a working definition that is especially helpful in our context of Faery realm, the UnderWorld, and the tasks of Faery Healing.

1. All beings in nature, corporeal or spiritual, are made up of combinations and rhythms of the Elements. Thus Faeries, Nature Spirits, humans, trees, plants, animals, fishes, insects, mountains, oceans, continents, telephone calling cards, chewing gum, and canned soft drinks are all composed of Elementals in varying patterns or sets of relationships. Some are highly active, some are relatively inactive.
2. Occasionally we will experience large Elementals, such as storms, fires, and earthquakes.
3. Elementals are not Faeries or Nature Spirits, but Faeries and Nature Spirits are often strongly elemental in their character.

Nature Spirits

So, Nature Spirits are ... what? As is so often the case, we can discover what something may be by discerning what it is not. Surely, they are not cutesy little cartoon things posturing upon cultivated, irradiated, and mutated cut flowers or lisping softly to us from the well-pruned toxin-laden trees of suburbia. I feel, sense, and commune with Nature Spirits as Spirits of Place – powerful zones of consciousness and energy in and of such places as a forest, a hill, or a river. They have distinct presence, powers, and perceptions, but they do not move around beyond their own boundaries. They are the spirits that the Ancients called *genii loci*, the geniuses or jinn of place.

By comparison, and of a different order, the spiritual forces of plants, flowers, and trees are collective entities within the natural world. Segments of these may live within, or comprise organs of, any specific Nature Spirit. Such collectives are found over huge areas, sometimes world wide, just like humans. Thus a grove of oak trees will be an organ of a Nature Spirit in a valley, but the collective of oak trees throughout the continent, even the planet, is an oak-entity in itself that is not confined in any smaller location, but is planetary in its being.

The Spirit of a Place, or Nature Spirit, might be compared broadly to the collective of a modern city: it has a unique identity of its own, and cannot depart from its rooted location, yet there are many independent beings within its field of energy and consciousness.

We could consider, as an example, that many humans and other creatures are part of the organism known to us as New York. It has a unique unmistakable identity and location, yet its individual inhabitants both are and are not part of it. This same simple spiritual law of Place, People, and Powers applies to mountains, forests, lakes, valleys, great oceans, planets, and stars.

So to return to the theme, Nature Spirits are complex entities made up of a totality of many other beings, and all involving Elementals. Just as humans, animals, and all living creatures are complex interactive beings made of other beings, so are Nature

Spirits. They are, however, rooted in place, be that place great or small, finite or cosmic in size and power. They are, in fact, matrices within which a collective develops and lives, even though members of that collective may travel far from their original home place, perhaps never to return.

The Racial Soul or Oversoul

This same idea of the collective that is founded in a location is also present in the rather confused concept of the Racial Soul or Racial Oversoul. The simplest definition of the Racial Soul is this: the soul of a race is, or was, originally united by the power of the land in which that race found its identity and coherence. No race is "pure," of course, but is broadly defined by certain distinctive characteristics associated with a land in which the people have lived for many generations (even if they do not live in that land now). Thus we would not easily confuse a Scot with a Swede, or a Native American with a Siberian, though each of these racial types share some things in common deep in their racial origins.

A race, as a collective, is not limited by that land, however, for its collective imprint will travel far within individuals that come from the original race. With time, these individuals and their descendants can, and often do, form a new collective, transformed by inter-action with the new land. Thus I am a Scot in America, like so many before me, and Scotland where I was born is in my soul. But I no longer live there and my descendants will become, appropriately, more and more American if they chose to live and procreate in this country.

At this stage we might consider that Ancestors can be of many races, even though we think of one or two only, from our obvious maternal or paternal lines. Some of our Ancestors may be Ancestors of skill rather than of blood, such as craftsmen, scientists, poets, musicians, or workers of Faery magic. At this level of ancestry, race is irrelevant.

What about the Faeries?

Traditionally, Faeries are said to be the first order of spiritual beings in the world, before humans existed. They, like all things, have Elementally-relative patterns. They are made up of Elementals, as we are, as all things on this planet are. But they, like us, are not solely Elementals. The whole is more than the sum of the parts. If you want a powerful magical phrase, that contains intense practical wisdom for magical work, paste this up where you can see it every day: *the whole is more than the sum of the parts.*

Faery beings will often tend strongly towards one Element, and traditionally are said be composed of one primary Element, two secondary Elements, and one almost dormant fourth Element. The living creatures, in comparison, have two dormant Elements and two active. A human has all Four Elements in potential balance, though usually one is somewhat weaker and one somewhat stronger. I leave you to decide how dormant they are after a meal of nutrition-free burgers and synthetic fries, washed down with a large drink replete with coloring, flavoring, and aspartame.

Thus a powerful Faery being of the ocean will be of Water more than any other Element, but it is not a Water Elemental. When one of the huge storms develops, short-lived Water Elementals grow in power, along with short-lived Air Elementals. Such Elementals are created by *movement*. The movement comes from the conscious-ness of the deep Titan beings of telluric or oceanic power, though to us it manifests as weather, earthquakes, or volcanic eruptions. The large vessels or Elementals, which we experience as dramatic and dangerous phenomena, are traditionally ridden by the Faery beings, which exalt in their wild Elemental power. So there is an energetic exchange, an interconnection, but the Faery beings are not the Elementals.

More significant is the long-standing tradition of the independence of Faery beings: many of them are not bound by place or elemental qualities, and can move and interact freely with considerable power. Thus they are not Nature Spirits or Elementals, though they may participate for some time in the life-cycle of certain places, as do humans, and all other living creatures. To put it more simply, Faery beings have independent personalities, aims, thoughts, practices, powers, sports, customs, loves, desires, and (surprise!) they do not use computers or cell phones. They are free spirits, after all.

Elementals, however, are utterly and only defined by elemental patterns beyond which they have no existence. Nature Spirits are defined by a complex interaction of power and place, a fusion of many varied energies of consciousness and vitality.

In Qabalistic tradition, the Elementals are said to be the result, the end product, of the consciousness and energy of universal angelic forces impinging upon our planet Earth, and thus generating a response. All living beings on the planet, physical and spiritual, partake of that response, being energized and, so to speak, given definition by the ceaseless Elemental dance of relationships.

In Conclusion

At the close of this first essay on Elementals, Nature Spirits, and Faeries, we might conclude that humans, living creatures, and Faeries are complex. They are made up of complex interactions of the primary Elements of Air, Fire, Water and Earth. They all have affinities to certain Elements more than to others: the fiery temperament in a flamenco dancer, the earthy strength of the male goat, the airy power of the trooping Faeries that cleanse the polluted cities as they pass, and so forth.

Nature Spirits are less complex, have less volition, but are immensely powerful through their continuing interaction with all the other beings and Elementals of a locus, of a place. This is why we feel distinct sensations in certain parts of the forest, in the mountains, or by the shore.

Elementals are usually within, and interacting with, all other forms, just the same as we have many smaller entities that comprise our organs, cells, and so forth. Occasionally large and temporary Elementals will grow together, from many, as natural forces build into major events such as storms, volcanic eruptions, tidal waves, and earthquakes. These active Elementals are comprised of all Four

Elements (like everything else) but with a potent preponderance of one main Element that is undeniable until it runs it course.

Hints for meditation

1. Try meditating on one single Element, and then discover how it exists in relationship to the others.
2. Seek to escape from sentimental images of Faeries, Nature Spirits, and Elementals. Explore the images, descriptions, and wisdom tales of our older, worldwide, ancestral traditions rather than the trite products of modern whimsy and commercialism.
3. Go out in the worst possible weather, on foot, without a Sony Walkman.

THE FAERY REALM

In this second essay of essential definitions, we will explore one of the main questions that is behind much of the material in this book, and in practical Faery magic in general.

What Is The Faery Realm, Who Or What Lives There, And Why Should We Concern Ourselves With It?

This is a question that I have addressed in a series of books over the last twelve years or more, and I am still discovering new answers.[1] Such answers are best discovered by practical experience of the Faery realm and the subtle energies therein, but we can go a long way towards a basic set of definitions in this article. We will also explore one of the more effective ways of experiencing the Faery consciousness and contact, so fasten your sporrans tightly. Please note that I am using the spelling "Faery" intentionally, to distinguish these spirit beings, widely reported in ancestral tradition, from the trivialized fairy images of modern entertainment. It is a small but helpful distinction.

The best way to begin is with the basic essential definitions handed down to us from folkloric and ancestral tradition. These are surprisingly simple, and are found in close variants worldwide. In this discussion, however, we will focus mainly on the British and European beliefs.[2] Why? Partly because these are the ones I know best, from traditions that I learned as a child and studied and expanded on as an adult. Also, because they act as a working model for the entire tradition. Once you have the grasped the basics, you can discover for yourself how they share a planetary tradition by researching comparative folklore, mythology, and ethnic magical traditions. It is the Faery Tradition that is at the foundation of all magic and spirituality worldwide, both as an ancestral source, and as a layer of deep consciousness occupied by many living beings.

So here is a brief question and answer sequence, which covers the absolutely fundamental basics of the Faery Tradition, by any name, in any culture.

Q: What is the Faery realm?

A: A prototypical land within and beneath the surface land; an archetype of the natural world; a timeless place of regeneration, beauty, and allure. Hmm, sounds good already, does it not?

Q: Who or what lives there?

A: The many Faery races, some human beings and certain Ancestors, and a host of creatures that are the spirit counterparts of animals, birds, fishes, insects, trees and plants, and the multitude of planetary life forms from the most minute to the most immense. There are also larger beings, deeper in, that we know less about. In old mythological traditions, these are called Titans (from Greek) or Giants (Latin and Germanic) and are often associated with mountains, volcanoes, fault lines, forests, glaciers, oceans, planetary zones, and planetary weather. As someone said to me: "It is never humans that rule the planet, it is the weather that rules it." Many of the occupants of the Faery realm are friendly towards their human cousins, but not all. Which is hardly surprising, when we consider how blindly destructive we have been. So maybe we need some caution and respect in this realm, rather than romantic wishful thinking?

Q: Why should we concern ourselves with the Faery realm?

A: Because it is a place of regeneration and transformation. As primal traditions advise us, we live in a complex interactive world of many interconnected beings, not in an artificial world of self-referring antagonistic humanity striving against everything else.

Such are the basics of the Faery Tradition as found in folklore, Faery tales, myths and legends worldwide. But there is more, a great deal more. The Faery Tradition is the foundation of all spirituality, religion, and all magic. Thus, if we are to transform our depleted and abused planet, it is a good tradition to explore, and the Faery realm is a good place to start. Faery Tradition is full of very detailed methods of relating to our Faery cousins, and to the spiritual creatures. Far from being a whimsical escapist tripping-through-the-daisies tradition, it deals with shape-changing, large powerful spirit beings, seeing and sensing at a distance, potent and dramatic healing arts, weather changing, prophecy, and sexual magic. Oh yes, sexual magic … which is only one reason why orthodox religions do not approve of Faery and human contacts. Both Christianity and Islam, for example, share the same prohibitions against consorting with Faeries and Jinn – against any communion with the ageless radiant ones who were in the world before humanity, and who will be in the world when humanity is gone.

Let us digress, for a moment, into the cozy realm of the skeptic, and pose a "what if" question. What if, despite much hardheaded materialistic life experience, there truly are spirits of the land and sea, invisible but powerful energetic forces that shape up as independent consciousness, often inaccessible to humans? Would you want to contact them, especially if you could help one another to improve the parlous state of our mutual world?

I would guess that the answer depends on how concerned we are about the health of the land, the continent, and the planet. If we are happy to merely plunder and pollute, then those Faeries can take a hike – who needs 'em anyway? But, if we are seriously considering any and all ways towards an increased awareness of the interaction, the holism, of all living beings on the planet, then this old ancestral world-view is at least worth a try, is it not?

If the Faery Tradition is about beings inherent within the subtle life of the land, just as we are inherent, and if it truly offers working methods whereby we can come into a friendly and creative relationship with such beings, then we may even feel a responsibility to try it, as well as an inspiration.

Very well: here is what you do…

The Well of Light

1.   Find a quiet place free of interruption. Now there is a major spiritual exercise in itself!
2.   Sit and be still, breathing gently. Draw in your random thoughts and feelings, and focus on the ground beneath you. If you are outdoors, sit on the grass or earth. If you are indoors, reach through the substance of the building down into the ground.
3.   With your inner vision, your imagination, see sense and feel a Well opening just in front of your feet. See a soft shifting light deep in the Well.
4.   Dive down into the Well in your inner vision and subtle senses. You emerge in a grassy place, lit from below by radiant Earth Light. You are at a tall standing stone in the middle of a wide grassy plain.
5.   Here you give a spontaneous gift, something that just comes into your hands, your vision, and your thoughts, to give unconditionally. You place it at the foot of the stone.
6.   Now beings come towards you from the Four Directions: some come softly, while others are more direct, even abrupt. Try to sense, see, and feel what they are like. They will take many forms.
7.   Commune in silence with them for a while: what intimations, hints, or questions do they offer you? What visions of the human world do you offer them?
8.   Now you return to the surface world. The rising radiance of the

Earth Light lifts you up, and you rise back out of the Well.

9.   You find yourself back in the surface world. For a few moments you sense it differently, as the Faery cousins see it and feel it. Gradually your human perceptions return.

10. Write a short account of what happened; make a song or a poem. Plant a seed, embrace a tree. Stroke a stone, merge with a flower through inhaling its perfume. Remember, the Faery realm is sexual, exchanging, and sharing subtle life forces. Embrace two trees.

Some Do's and Don'ts

There are many prohibitions or taboos in the older Faery Traditions. Here are a few that apply today, with some reasons for them. You will probably know of others, or discover them in Faery tales and folklore.[3]

1.   Never cut any flowers, nor have cut flowers in your dwelling. Why? The flowers are the sexual organs of the plant and you mutilate and kill them when you cut them. How would you feel?

2.   Leave small tasty sweet offerings in the same place each day: nothing too lavish, but high-energy stuff of all sorts. Throw it away the next day, for it has had the subtle energy taken from it by the spirit or Faery beings. They do not require the substance as we do. They love sugar and chocolate, just as we do, but presumably do not suffer so much from its over-use. Be cautious about leaving them whisky or strong beer. Traditionally Faeries love alcohol, but can become rowdy and even potentially dangerous. I report all of this from direct experience, not from a source book, though much of it is found in early texts such as *The Secret Commonwealth of Elves, Fauns and Fairies*, which we will refer to in several places throughout this book. If you want to read my edition, with a commentary, there is a free version at <u>www.dreampower.com</u>. You will also find some quotes in our later chapters.

3.   If you are offered food or drink in the Faery realm, *take it!* Traditionally we are told not to take it, which means *take it quickly* before they withdraw the courteous and wonderful offer. To

partake of food and drink is to share the subtle forces of the world in which that food and drink was made. This is the secret behind our human offerings to the Faery races, which is discussed in Chapter 5 on *Offerings*.

4.   Be cautious with repeated visions or subtle experiences of sexual exchange with Faery lovers – not because it is bad or wrong, but because (like all sensuous activity) it can become highly addictive. Moderation is a word seldom found in the Faery vocabulary.

5.   Never cut branches or plants with steel or iron. You should pick or pull by hand if you have to. Everyone debates this tradition, but I think it means simply that you must have loving contact to break a branch with your hand, rather than with a cold unfeeling blade. Gardeners all know how deeply satisfying it is to pull weeds rather than cut them up. That is the very essence of it: touching and pulling, not slicing and dividing.

6.   Always keep any promises that you may make in the Faery realm. The spirit of intention is everything. The worst thing you could do is to break a promise made in that archetypal and sacred place.

7.   Always be respectful to the Cousins: they are not "helpers." Join with me, sisters and brothers, in repudiating and despising the popular notion that Faeries are "helpers." How insulting this human-centric statement is to Faery allies, cousins, and co-walkers. I suppose the Faeries must, therefore, call us humans the "hinderers."

8.   Expect the unexpected.

TITANS AND GIANTS

As we move deeper into the Faery realm, we encounter large powers and larger beings, often hidden deep in the lands and seas, yet they affect our lives profoundly. These are known in tradition as Titans and Giants. In this essay we will explore some of the basic traditions concerning these larger spiritual entities of our living world. Let us begin, therefore, with three relevant questions, as most things come in threes.

1. What are Titans and Giants?
2. Why should we bother with them?
3. How might we relate to them?

There is a complex interaction between Titans, Giants, and other life forms, though often we are unconscious of it. This becomes clear, however, as we explore Questions 1 & 2. Some of the answers to Question 3 will be proposed, in part, at the end of this article. I say "in part," because the answers require doing, rather than reading about. But first things first: What are Titans and Giants?

The roots of all answers are found in ancestral mythic tradition. In traditions associated with Titans and Giants, we discover how stories of their existence and their role have developed. Worldwide, there are three classes of primal stories about such beings (three, of course!). This article refers mainly to European sources as the working models for all such stories, in any culture, worldwide.

Titans and Giants are, essentially, spiritual beings. However, their bodies are zones of the planet or continents, or of the oceans, mountains, volcanoes and vast weather patterns. This is why tradition attributes tidal waves, earthquakes, eruptions, and storms to the actions of Titans or Giants.

Three Classes of Myth Concerning Titans or Giants

1. The first class is that of creation myths, in which bodies of vast beings are dismembered or willingly sacrificed to create the world.[4] Some typical examples are Ymir the ice Giant whose skull makes the vault of the sky in Norse creation myth, the dismemberment of Ra in Egyptian myth, and the ancient Qabalistic tradition of the Adam Cadmon, or universal primal being. These are each telling the same story in different ways.
2. The second class or group of myths, with many variants world-wide, describes mentoring. Mentoring myths have been given less attention than creation myths in modern literature, but are especially significant for us today if we seek to consciously work

with Titans and Giants to redeem the damage done by humanity to the living planet. In many cultural and mythic traditions, large beings are described as mentors of humanity teaching arts, science, mathematics, music, agriculture and so forth. We often forget that the ancestral cultures had no separation between creative arts and magical arts, between sciences and magical or spiritual sciences. All forms of human endeavor had a spiritual and sacro-magical role.

A typical mentoring myth is the ancient Greek, or pre-Greek, story of Atlas, the Titan who founds Atlantis, and whose sons become kings of civilization. Another is found in the Old Testament, and in the Book of Enoch, wherein Giants intermarry with humans, and teach them skills, arts, and magic. In Celtic tradition certain immortal or semi-divine beings come into the world and teach humanity the arts of civilization; they are often described as being of giant size. Examples include members of the Tuatha de Danaan in Irish legend, and the Welsh Titan Bran, who (in the legend of Branwen, daughter of Llyr in The Mabinogion) wades the Irish sea, bridges the river Liffy with his body, and "carries the poets and musicians upon his back." The father of Bran and Branwen is Llyr, god of the Atlantic Ocean, the Celtic Poseidon. Poseidon was the Greek god of earthquakes and tidal waves, older than the Olympians and traditionally the god of ancient Atlantis.[5]

3.   The third group is myths of destruction. These balance the creation myths, with myths of mentoring in the center, the place of harmony. Perhaps the best known examples are in Norse mythology, where the Giants seek to bring Ragnarok, and the winter that ends the world, toppling the gods and goddesses of Asgard. This theme is identical to Greek legends of the Titans who raise storms, earthquakes, and tidal waves in their war with the Olympian deities, whom they are said to oppose. In a more obscure but no less significant Celtic tradition, we find warring and destructive Giants who change the shape of the land. This myth comes from the *Prophecies of Merlin*, a 12th century text that contains a wealth of Breton and Welsh bardic and druidic imagery.[6]

In the older Greek mythic traditions, we find that the Titans were originally deities of the seven planets (Moon, Sun, Mercury, Venus,

Mars, Jupiter, and Saturn). They descended into the body of the Earth, and the Olympian deities took their places. Robert Graves suggests[7] that the typifying of the Titans as "bad guys" hostile to the (sometimes) good deities such as Zeus, Hera, Apollo, Hermes, and Aphrodite was propaganda. We find similar propaganda in other texts and myths, whenever an old form of religion or spiritual tradition is replaced by a more recent one. The stories are not fabricated, but well established myths are slowly molded to a propagandist cause. In Celtic tradition, the Gaels in Scotland and Ireland told that the Faery races were angels fallen out of Heaven with Lucifer, and now embodied in the Earth. This is a Christianized retelling of an older tradition, similar to that of the Titans. Such stories, and many other similar legends worldwide, tell of spiritual forces that move between the planets of the solar system, affecting life here on Earth. Some of this becomes clear when we explore the role of Titans and Giants in connection with the forces of volcanoes, weather, and continental movement. As modern science asserts, these large changes are affected by our planetary orbit and by its relationship to solar and other planetary forces. These all act upon, and interact with, our earth's oceans, plates, and the deep telluric or UnderWorld fires, the star-stuff in the heart of Earth.

Thus the three groups of myths tell us much about Titans and Giants, with interwoven subtle implications: Creation, Development (mentoring) and Destruction. The creation and destruction are on a large scale, usually planetary, sometimes cosmic; land and planet are often interchangeable with cosmos in primal myths. The development or mentoring theme tells us of conscious care and attention given to the relationship between differing orders of life, especially through the role of humanity.

A good example of this is the myth of the Titan Cronos, from the writing of Hesiod, available in many translations. In this Greek legend a vast spiritual being rules over the Golden Age in which all beings live in harmony together. Cronos is described as the mentor of humanity in a world of primal and idyllic peace.

First of all the deathless gods who dwell on Olympus made a golden race of mortal men who lived in the time of Cronos when he was reigning in heaven. And they lived like gods without sorrow of heart, remote and free from toil and grief: miserable age rested not on them; but with legs and arms never failing they made merry with feasting beyond the reach of all evils. When they died, it was as though they were overcome with sleep, and they had all good things; for the fruitful earth unforced bare them fruit abundantly and without stint. They dwelt in ease and peace upon their lands with many good things, rich in flocks and loved by the blessed gods. (Hesiod, Works and Days, ll. 109-120)

Back to Creation, Development and Destruction. The Titans and Giants are forces that shape the planet. They are associated with coming into being, with development of life on Earth, and with the transformative (to us destructive) forces. Far from being crude or ignorant stories to "explain why we have earthquakes," myths of Titans and Giants are models of relationship. They tell us about the large forces in our planet, and most important, they tell us that such forces also shape humanity. But of course they do, for we live within the land and planet, and are indeed shaped, developed, and transformed by our relationship with them. Today we are in an age of massive climate changes which many scientists think are the result of human irresponsibility and greed. This could be described by the Mythic model: we have lost our living relationship to the land and planet, embodied on a large scale by the Titans and Giants as planetary organs. Their response is transformation, destruction, and eventual regeneration and rebalancing.

This raises some important and even uncomfortable questions for our theme, and practice, of Faery Healing and Earth Healing; much of our deepest work has to be done with the Titans and related larger UnderWorld beings. We will go into this idea of working with the large entities in our later chapters, especially in connection with the Well of Light, and the Mystery of the Double Rose.

Consider this: it only needs the weather patterns to change a little more, and the entire viability of human culture will be threatened or rendered void. We have triggered planetary weather changes through pollution, industrialization, and indifference to long-term patterns in favor of short-term profits. It only needs the volcanic, telluric patterns to become a little more active to wipe out major centers of population, and change the pattern of human inhabitation. We have triggered such activity with our underground and undersea nuclear explosions. Furthermore we have a potent legend that warns us about such arrogance in the legend of Atlantis (described in the works of Plato), founded by the Titan Atlas, but ultimately destroyed by human folly.

We are living in a time when the relationship between humanity and the Titans and Giants is changing, in part due to human folly. I say "in part," because on a mythic scale, our folly results from the Mentoring described earlier – we take the wisdom of the Titans, of the UnderWorld, and misapply it for selfish unethical ends. So the destructive phase is not merely a humano-centric problem, it is part of a bigger picture.

As I mentioned earlier, the answers to questions 1 and 2 (Why should we bother with Titans and Giants, and how might we relate to them?) are intertwined, and by exploring who or what the Titans and Giants are, we have also explored why we might wish to have a better relationship with them.

Why Should We Bother With Them?

Firstly, we are within them all the time. Those of us who live in California, especially on the coasts on the fault lines, know that as a daily truth that cannot be lightly dismissed. This applies to many of the unstable areas of the world. And the whole human world is within, and, like it or not, utterly ruled by the planetary weather. Have you ever thought of that, reader? I am thinking of it more often nowadays. We are all within, and subject to, the larger planetary telluric forces which give rise to weather, tidal waves, earthquakes, and volcanoes. But they also give rise to life itself: new organisms appear in the ocean depths where the UnderWorld fires meet the deep waters. Indeed, new life forms are being discovered down there by our biologists. This is the root of creation, the power of the Titans working to make life.

So, to ignore them is possible, and millions of humans certainly do just that, but it is not possible to live without them. Can we understand their patterns? Yes, to a certain extent through our sciences. But at a deeper level we have to work in meditation, vision, and through altered consciousness. As we are already within the Titans and Giants, for they are the vast organs or zones of the land and planet, we must be able to interact with them consciously – but how? This brings us to our third question:

How Might We Relate To Them?

1. *Through an altered perspective* – I would propose that first we relate through a much needed sense of humility and altered perspective. The grossly humano-centric stance of our modernist culture is destroying us at no uncertain pace. Diseases, pollution, indifference and rapacious greed are wiping us out ... yet we think we are going faster and faster, and getting better and better. While we might consider the theme of this book, Faery Healing, to be focused on curing diseases or injuries through working with Faery allies, the deeper Earth Healing comes only through a transformed relationship with the Titans, Giants, and UnderWorld powers that are the sources of all planetary life, including humans, Faeries, and living creatures.

2. *Through the weather* – If we meditated for three minutes each day on the weather, and how the weather binds and looses all life, including us humans, we would take a small step towards relating to the Titans and Giants.

3. *Through the mountains* – If we meditated upon the mountains, as our Ancestors did, we would be opening our awareness to the big picture. What are mountains, after all? Are they just

an annoying feature that we have to tunnel into to drive through or fly over, or are they the spine, bones, and core of the land? Yes, I know, no one has time to travel to the mountains. We are too busy sitting in traffic jams or trying to get our computers to download so-called time-saving free music. But if we cannot travel physically, we can go there in vision and meditation. Try it, it works powerfully. There are many methods for deep spiritual communion and healing in this book. If you were to work with only one or two of them regularly, it would change your life, and eventually, the entire world.

4. *Through Faery cousins and allies* – Now we are coming to the more esoteric and specific traditions. Our Faery cousins and allies, and the spirit creatures as co-walkers, will help us build a living relationship with the Titans and Giants. They act, not only as go-betweens, but as part of an organic network in the true sense, being composed of interrelated organs of consciousness. This technique is featured in many of my own workshops and books.[8] In essence, it consists of meditating upon the Faery allies, and requesting them to make contact with the larger beings, the Titans and Giants, then participating in that contact. It brings a stream of consciousness that is non-verbal, not limited by artificial time, and deeply regenerative.

In Conclusion

There is much to think about in the theme of Titans and Giants; we have hardly touched upon it in this short essay. I hope, at least, to have offered you some inspiration, some new perspectives. And, of course, some hope that we can, and will, come into a new and harmonious relationship with our living planet. To go further, you can work with the methods described in our later chapters. But before you do so, I would recommend reading through the rest of the essays on Essential Definitions. There are two more.

UNDERWORLD SPIRITUALITY

In this essay we explore the basic nature of UnderWorld spirituality, an idea that is gaining wider attention as more people turn to earth-based magic and religion. To do any Faery magic or Faery Healing, we have to have some foundation in our understanding regarding the UnderWorld.

There are two main aspects of UnderWorld spirituality and magic: Transformation and Regeneration. These have been the two pillars of the UnderWorld traditions worldwide for millenniums, regardless of culture, religion, race, or geographical location. (I use the spelling UnderWorld intentionally, to refer to a realm of energy and consciousness, so that we do not think of organized crime under the surface of the planet!)

During the 21st century, at least in the West, we are finally emerging from a long suppressive phase of group consciousness, in which the UnderWorld was equated with evil or, at least undesirable, earth forces. Why are such earth forces undesirable? Because, we have been told repeatedly that they are Below rather than Above. It takes a long time for the collective psyche to emerge from religious manipulation, and we find this same divisive pattern inherent in much of our current spiritual revival. Yet, I would propose that such a naïve dualistic argument fails, even in terms of common sense. Above and Below are illusions fostered by gravity. Go far enough Below and you come to the sky again. It is the journey through the UnderWorld that leads us to the Stars and liberates us from antagonistic dualism.

More simply, all growing things are nourished from Below: our very existence on Earth fails without the life forces that rise from Below. A tree cannot survive without roots, and the circulation of energies from Below is the foundation of all growth in our world. In the spiritual traditions we discover that truths of nature are also truths of spirit. If we refer back to ancestral times, no more than a century or so, we find folkloric traditions of the Faery and UnderWorld powers in Western culture. Some of these have been discussed in the earlier essays in this chapter. A little further back again, and we begin to find UnderWorld spirituality at the core of the oldest traditions, such as those of the Celts, the Norse and Germanic peoples, the Greeks, and the Romans, and very substantially in the myths of the Native American nations, both north and south. Far from being outmoded old junk and superstition, such traditions provide a working model of relationship between humanity and the land, the planet, couched in terms of gods and goddesses, and practiced as ceremonies and magical techniques. Today we would call this Environmental Magic. But in the past there was no "environment," there was only Life. And life begins and ends in the nourishing, regenerative, transformative depths of the Earth – in the UnderWorld.

Where Is The UnderWorld?

So where, exactly, is this deeper UnderWorld that our Ancestors understood to be the source of life? It is somewhat below the Faery realm, though it includes the Faery realm, and it also includes collective ancestral memories. I will rephrase that for clarity: the Faery realm is that spiritual dimension where humanity intersects with all plants and living creatures, with the elemental forces of sea, wind, earth, and fire. This is where the Faery races are found, somewhere between the surface world and the deeper planetary forces. Indeed, they act as go-betweens or mediators. The UnderWorld is deeper than the Faery realm alone, and its spiritual forces are mediated to us by the older gods and goddesses, the Titans and Giants, and the vast planetary being, of which they are all organs, parts, dreams, and inhabitants.

In ancestral sacro-magical practices, the UnderWorld was often the realm of the dark goddess. She brought transformation, as she was, and still is, the goddess of destruction and regeneration. This dark goddess, known by many names worldwide, personifies the transformative forces of the planet. And yes, these are forces that we can and do work with. I say, "do work with" because we interact with such forces continuously, as part of our life on Earth. We could not exist without the dark goddess, by whatever name she chooses to be called. There is a difference, of course, between intentional work and unconscious interaction. If we work with these planetary UnderWorld forces intentionally, the transformative process is greatly enhanced and accelerated.

This is one of the so-called "secrets" of the old magical traditions: if you consciously interact with the planetary forces of the UnderWorld, you will become transformed. First comes destruction of the false self of delusion, and then comes regeneration of the true self unalloyed by temporary personality.

How do we get into the UnderWorld?

For many years now I have been using a simple visionary technique for people to access the power of the UnderWorld, through the image of the dark goddess. Various forms of this have been published in my books, and are now widely used in workshops and individual spiritual work. Friends and fellow esoteric pioneers first undertook this method in the 1970s. In the early 1980s, it was given its first public use at gatherings in Hawkwood College, Stroud, England, sponsored and led by Gareth Knight (author of many books on Qabalah and white magic). Since those early days thousands of people have used this method to enter the UnderWorld, seek transformation, and safely return again. Here is the shortest version; try it for yourself:

The Cave and Pool Vision

Sit somewhere where you will not be disturbed.

Using your imagination, see, sense, and feel before you a spiral stair descending down a well. It leads into the UnderWorld. Feel yourself descend that stair, spiraling down and down. You leave the surface world behind. At last you come into a small cave where the feeling is one of peace and stillness, in the regenerative calm shadows lit only by a tiny lamp hanging from the roof. In the center of the cave is a pool of dark still water.

On the other side of the pool, sense, see, and feel the presence of the dark goddess. You must cross through the pool and give her a gift. Your gift is unconditional and spontaneous. Whatever it may be, you give it freely and with no thought of a return.

Having given your gift, commune awhile with the goddess in silence. When you sense that it is time, you return across the pool and climb back up the stairs to the place where you began your vision. Sit still for a few moments and readjust to the surface world again. (Keep a written record of your experiences, and do this once or twice a week, no more is necessary.)

In Conclusion

If you stay with this very simple exercise, you will find that it builds strongly and that you can easily enter into it. With practice you may ask the goddess questions, or she may offer you insights and tasks. A wide variety of experiences arise from this vision, which allows our subtle energies to interact with those flowing beneath the surface of the land, those of the UnderWorld. In a time of environmental crisis, every effort that we make to enter into a new relationship with the land and the planet is of immense value, no matter how small that effort may be. With this simple exercise we are not merely restating ancestral spirituality through a modern vision; we are participating in a realm of consciousness and energy that has been ignored by materialistic humanity for too long. Now is the time to transform and regenerate our vision of the planet as a living being, and ourselves as part of that being. This is our task, not merely one of self-development, but of self-healing and Earth Healing.

These essays have set the scene and introduced you to some of the practical work involved in the Faery and UnderWorld traditions. We are now ready to move on to the more detailed and in-depth material on Faery Healing and Earth Healing that are the main themes of this book.

Notes:

1. *Earth Light*; *Power Within the Land*; *The Living World of Faery*; *The UnderWorld Initiation*: Various editions 1985-1990, R.J. Stewart. Most recent US editions: Mercury Publishing, 1998/9

2. *Fairy Faith in Celtic Countries*, W.Y. Evans-Wentz; *The Faery Encyclopedia*, Kathleen Briggs. There are many editions of these major reference books. You can often find them second hand by using online book searches.

3. *Robert Kirk, Walker Between the Worlds, a new edition of The Secret Commonwealth of Elves, Fauns and Fairies*. From the 17th Century notebook of the Rev. Robert Kirk of Aberfoyle. Edited with commentary by R.J. Stewart, first published by Element Books, UK, 1989.

4. See *Elements of Creation Myth*, R.J. Stewart, Element Books, 1991.

5. For the Celtic stories see *Celtic Gods, Celtic Goddesses*, R.J. Stewart, Blandford Press, 1986

6. See *Merlin: The Prophetic Vision and Mystic Life*, R.J. Stewart, Penguin Arkana, 1986. You can find an online edition of the Prophecies, with a commentary, at www.dreampower.com.

7. *Greek Myths*, Robert Graves, various editions.

8. *Earth Light* and *Power Within the Land*, R.J. Stewart, 1991 reprinted Mercury Publishing, 1998.

2. The Faery Races,
Their Appearances, and Inner Contact

This chapter offers a short summary of the esoteric or "secret" aspects of the Faery and UnderWorld tradition, describing briefly the main Faery races or orders of being, and how their nature is presented in ancestral tradition. The basis for all of our practical work begins with tradition and myth, as these contain rich veins of wisdom preserved for us by the ancestors. From tradition and myth, we progress to direct practical work, using the ancestral lore as a starting point and touchstone for comparison. This chapter is not intended as an academic text on folklore, or an analysis of mythology. Some sources are listed in the Bibliography and in the Chapter Notes for those readers who wish to research literary material from the ancient world, mythology, or collections of folklore.

Nowadays there is much confusion and commercialization regarding the Faery races. Yet their nature is well described in all spiritual traditions worldwide, and it is easy to dispose of the nonsense that is found in entertainment and pseudo-spirituality. We can begin with the traditions, and then progress to meeting the Faery races directly. After a short exploration of the wealth of information in tradition and myth, we will progress to describing the appearances of Faery beings, and how we may work with these appearances in direct Inner Contact.

WHAT DO THE TRADITIONS TEACH US?

One of the most important, yet often overlooked traditions is found worldwide. It teaches that the Faery races (by whatever name they may be known in differing lands and cultures) are the primal beings of this world – not of the world as it is now, but of its prototype or innocent first form.

We may gain some helpful metaphysical insights from an esoteric perspective, as well as from inner contacts through meditation on the primal tradition described above. These are similar in many ways to statements found in a very significant document, the *Secret Commonwealth of Elves Fauns, and Fairies*, a hand written note-book of Faery evidence, experiences, and conclusions by the Rev. Robert Kirk in the 1690s.

Our consensual world is devolved from that of the Faery races, through a process of materialization. Thus we are of the Surface world, and they are of the world Below. We are living on the hardened skin of the world, while they live in the malleable tissue that forms its foundation. This tissue holds its form in shape, but sometimes sheds and regenerates the skin.

Together, the many Faery races embody and mediate the life and death forces of the planet: the smaller beings are hive-like, forming huge collectives. These are the beings often called "devas" or "nature" spirits, although this is somewhat vague and incorrect. Most beings in the Faery realm are not nature spirits or elementals. While in the past, the differences and connections were known and understood, today they are lost and generalized beyond usefulness. (See Chapter 1: *Essential Definitions*)

The largest beings are the organs of consciousness of great planetary entities: oceans, mountain ranges, and continental zones. These are the Titans or Giants of ancestral mythology. They also have deep connections to stellar patterns, especially in the relative and synchronistic relationships that occur with alignments, rising and setting of star-groups, and long-term cosmic patterns of stellar relationships.

Of special interest to us, and with relevance to our work, are those in-between the smallest and greatest. They form the general orders of Faery beings that may, and often do, work with humans. They may seem to be human-like, though this is often a form of communicative mimicry, well described in the old Faery traditions.

Some Faery beings still live exclusively in the Dream of the World, in that primal expanding planetary life-force and dreaming consciousness that creates and generates the surface world and its living beings. They have no wish to be involved with us, yet they are not hostile to us. Indeed, they are often unaware of our externalizing, materializing, and devolved surface world, which has moved far from the primal Dream of the World. This movement is due substantially to humans, but there are also long-term forces of planetary change making slow inevitable contributions to the shifting relationship between the Surface World and the UnderWorld and Faery realm.

While some Faeries have no dealings with us, others have a deep and abiding interest in humans, and are committed to working with us. They are, at least in part, released from the Dream of the World; yet they still partake of its forces. A small number are free of the Dream entirely, thus being free from their tie to one location or land, and are highly mobile and powerful. These often act as mentors to humanity, in the traditions of Faery magic and spiritual arts and disciplines. In mythic terms, these mentors could be said to correspond to specific Titans, as if they are organs or aspects of the Titans, as independent components of the greater Titan awareness. Hence, we have the legends of the Titans (such as Atlas and Cronos) who educated early humans in the arts and sciences, and of the Giants (as in the Jewish and Christian traditions) who taught subtle arts to humans and sought to influence human evolution. Once they are free of the Dream of the World, such beings act as mediators of the planetary forces of change and evolution, perceiving the Dream without being bound by it. These great ones sense, see, and feel the connection between Earth and Stars, and form an important bridge between our world and the greater cosmos.

In old Celtic tradition, they are said to be the angels that fell out of Heaven with Lucifer (in a Christianized legend). This story is a dogmatic rationalization of an ancient creation myth: Light from the spiritual dimensions "falls" into the body of the planet, and many lesser but powerful spiritual beings move with the Light. Later, these are called Lucifer and fallen angels by Christians, or Iblis and the jinn by Muslims.

Regrettably, such legends, myths, and spiritual teachings have become debased and abused in modern interpretations (especially to make money) wherein the mentors are said to be aliens from other galaxies. No one seems to consider how demeaning and ignoble this trite nonsense is: it says, in effect, that humans on planet Earth were just ignorant semi-apes until aliens came along, and bred them and taught them. Such ideas are merely a twisted variant of Darwinian materialism combined with a post-Christian conditioning regarding a human inability to do anything worthwhile (i.e., sinfulness).

APPEARANCES AND INNER CONTACTS

At this point, we can begin to explore some of the classic and typical appearances, or presentations of inner contact, in the Faery Tradition. What does this mean? It means that who and what they are, and how they seem or appear, are not always the same. When you work with any spiritual contact, it is the sense of what they *feel like* that is of more significance to us as humans than the visual appearance. Put more simply, it is just like the human world. A glamorous appearance may mask a tawdry and petty interior, be it a house or a human. Much folk wisdom and many Faery tales are based on these sorts of truths. But the traditional tales take it further than down-home wisdom, for they often describe very specific entities and energies, rather than merely confirm psychological truisms.

The legend of Beauty and the Beast is a classic example of polarity magic between a human (Beauty) and a powerful spirit being (the Beast), just as much as it is a parable about human nature and appearances. Some aspects of Beauty and the Beast are paralleled in the initiatory Scottish ballad of Tam Lin, for both Tam Lin and the Beast are rationalized as ex-humans, transformed in some way due to their actions. Yet, both are more than human, and many of the dynamics of practical Faery magic are found in the calling, communing, and final redemption of both Tam Lin and the Beast. In short, both Faery tales teach us that appearances are not all, for *behind any appearance there are many levels of consciousness and being.*

This is especially true in the Faery realm, for the forms that we discern are often built from images in our own imagination. This is a subtle and powerful teaching that must not be underestimated or rationalized into a psychological mold. The images that arise to our inner senses when we are in contact with Faeries are not fantasies, nor are the Faery races themselves merely products of the human imagination or the so-called unconscious mind.

What arises in inner contact is that a Faery being, which has a pure form of its own, will resonate with an image or memory in the human psyche, the mind, and thus dress itself in that image. The process may be automatic or it may be intentional. This depends on the skill of both the Faery contact and the human contact. The dressing, appearances, and mimicry were well known in the old Faery tradition, where an entire repertoire of postures, colors, clothing, and attributes were once known. The Rev. Robert Kirk, in his notebook of 1692, *The Secret Commonwealth of Elves, Fauns, and Fairies*, describes this tradition briefly. Whereas the tradition of appearances was already on its way to being a lost art in Kirk's day, its principles are founded on the idea of resonant images ... something that holds meaning for both the human and the Faery. We should not see this as masquerading or deception, but have to work with it, as humans, to come to the inner understanding of the process. Once we have done so, Faery communication and communion becomes not only easier, but also highly empowered.

The How and Why of Appearances

The following summary deals with Faery appearances, but the

principles will apply to any and all Inner Contacts, regardless of spiritual, magical, or religious tradition, since the Faery tradition is at the foundation of all spirituality and magic worldwide. Not as a dogma, of course, but as a foundational aspect of consciousness on planet Earth. So the simple ground rules outlined here will also be helpful for working with other Inner Contacts.

There are some basic groups or categories that are helpful for the human student, magician, or Faery practitioner to remember. This list is not intended to be definitive, but to give broad groupings that enable us, as humans, to have some relative sense of what happens with Faery and inner contact.

1. Fixed Appearances
These are known and described in tradition, and remain fairly constant. Thus, in a religion or mythic tradition, the gods and goddesses have certain relatively Fixed Appearances, established through time and usage, and vitally important in their interaction with humans.

The High Faery Tradition – This Faery tradition has its Fixed Appearances and known personae: in many Faery tales there is a courtly ambience, with the Faery Queen and King, the Warriors, the Maidens, the Poet and Prophet, and the Herald. These all come from a vaguely medieval zone within the collective, semi-historical dream consciousness. They embody *functions* within Fixed Appearances. In the medieval historical manuscripts of Celtic legends, drawing upon much earlier oral traditions, we find that the ambience of the supernatural or Faery realm is pre-medieval. The classic examples are the descriptions of the Tuatha de Danaan in the Irish *Book of Invasions*, where we might think of the appearances as embodying both magical and historical images from an earlier era, perhaps the Bronze Age, with weapons of bone and bronze, costumes of crystal and gold, and highly stylized imagery that merges into metaphysical description. All of these, within what we might call the High Faery Tradition, find their way into inner contact.

The Low Faery Tradition – In this branch, the appearances are those beloved of popular entertainment and whimsy today: the pooka, the leprechaun, the banshee, the shimmering maiden, the small winged Faery, the ogre, the giant, the crone, the seductive maiden, the seductive male lover, the seal being, and so forth. Yet, if we look at the original tales of this low, or folkloric, tradition, we find that the dwarf and the leprechaun, far from being cute little guys with pointy shoes, are powerful and fearsome spiritual entities, associated with the geomantic or telluric forces of land and earth. The Low Faery Tradition has been hijacked and trivialized, especially with regard to visual appearances in film, television, and illustration.

As with all inner contacts, we have to consider function, and traditional descriptions of actions and functions, rather than be trapped into a stereotype of human-centric whimsy. If we do this, we will find great riches and resources in the appearances of the Low Faery Tradition.

Beware of false descriptions!!! There are many superficial books currently on the market that claim to describe Faery beings, usually with big smiles, green coats or red hats, or gauzy wings and skimpy dresses. These are the products of fantasy, and are the most superficial level of appearances. In Faery tradition what you see is *not* what you get, especially if you have a store of whimsical images in your mind. These whimsical images will be populated by Faery beings if necessary, but it would be better for you to study and attune to the Fixed Appearances from the older traditions. Examples of the High and Low Faery Traditions may be found in many source texts.

2: Fluid Appearances

Beyond, behind, and below the well-known Fixed Appearances from tradition are the deeper forms, which we might call Fluid Appearances. These are usually related to function, so a large powerful being that often has a Fixed Appearance as a small being will show as such in your inner vision and to your inner senses, but in a changeable and strange manner. You might see large eyes, or parts of a huge shifting pattern, for example. These deeper forms are often unusual and sometimes intensely beautiful or unsettling to a human. They relate more to the pure energy and consciousness of the Faery being than to a human-centric collective of images, such as are known in the Fixed Appearances. There are two levels of Fluid Appearances in the Faery realm.

The Lesser Appearances – At this first level of Fluid Appearances you will find those theriomorphic forms that combine, paradoxically, human and animal, human and bird, insect, or fish. You will also find combination beings: an entity that is made up of two or more others in subtle relationship. These Lesser Appearances will often change shape, giving rise to the many stories traditions and superstitions about shape shifting in the Faery realm. If you establish a good working relationship at this level, your Faery contact will often remain in one specific appearance for practical purposes. Because we use the term "lesser," it does not mean weaker or less significant. It only means that they are lesser in size and consciousness than the next category of Fluid Appearances.

The Greater Appearances – This second level of Fluid Appearances includes those large beings that embody the energies and consciousness of the mountains, regions of land, of a lake or river, of a volcano, or of an island in the ocean. They may also be the greater entity that utters or births smaller entities, for some Faery contacts are large and powerful hive beings. These greater appearances will often work through emissaries, where one stands for many, and the many ultimately stand for the greater entity of which they are a collective.

The Formless and Shining Ones

The deepest level of Faery contact is found deep in the body of the land and planet. These are often formless, and are sensed and felt rather than seen. They are also known as the Shining Ones, which are vast radiant conscious entities that are at the core of the planetary Being. The Shining Ones often appear to us as geometric or abstract shapes of light, with complex networks of interconnection. In the deepest teachings of the Faery tradition, it is the Shining Ones that dream all life forms manifesting to the surface world of nature.

Our communion with these greater entities is often through intermediaries: the Threefold Alliance of human, Faery, and living creature is the classic practical example. But there are other intermediaries, especially among the Greater Appearances. In practice, the Faery contacts will make a line or network of communion if the human contact is unable to come into direct consciousness with the deeper levels. This is a helpful process, and there are many magical arts based upon it.

The Other Ones

There are also many obscure UnderWorld entities that are associated with forces of transformation, destruction, and regeneration. They have very little connection with humanity, though we can work with them through intermediaries. These Others are especially valuable to us in the more advanced forms of Faery Healing, which deals with healing the rifts in the subtle forces of the land or sea, and the greater task of Earth Healing.

The Go-Betweens

Go-Betweens are transhuman, or ex-human, beings in the Faery realm. Traditional examples include the prophet and poet Thomas Rhymer, and the Reverend Robert Kirk: both are known historical persons (not mythic or traditional characters), and both are said to be actively present in the Faery realm, mediating between outer humanity and Faery consciousness and Faery beings. Most Go-Betweens are not known to history, of course, and you can make contact with them at the Crossroads, and through the Well of Light as described in our other empowered visions.

This short outline of the Faery Races sets the scene for many of the later chapters, and you will find that much of it comes into better perspective when you practice the techniques described in the following chapters. Ultimately, we learn about the Faery races through direct contact and communion, rather than from definitions in a book. Furthermore, as discussed earlier, popular definitions can be misleading and trivial, and must be examined ruthlessly for sentiment, whimsy, and escapism.

In our next chapter, we will move on to discovering your Aptitudes for Faery Healing, and exploring how you many activate these, and use them in practice.

3. The Seven Aptitudes for Faery Healing

The Seven Aptitudes are natural abilities that manifest in individuals in connection with Faery Healing. The Aptitudes also relate to other Faery and UnderWorld arts and skills, and we will discuss some of these relationships as we proceed. As our main theme is Faery Healing, however, we will not be able to explore all the complex interconnections in detail. Much of the background material can be found in the earlier books in this series: *The UnderWorld Initiation*, *Earth Light*, and *Power Within the Land*, or in *The Living World of Faery*.

The Seven Aptitudes are inherent abilities or potentials, although they are usually unrealized. They may need intense discipline and hard work for some people, while in others they simply flow forth when attention is given to them. Discovering that you have one or more of the inherent Aptitudes (and we all have at least one of them) is only the beginning: they have to be accessed, developed, and usually need to be attuned through dedicated inner work. There are many hints in tradition about how to develop and attune the Aptitudes. In this book, we present and explore new modern methods that have grown out of the older traditional material through experiment, personal experience, and insight.

WHAT ARE THE SEVEN APTITUDES?

The Seven Aptitudes are a set of mutually interacting abilities or talents, which are defined for us by the way they manifest. A simple list would be as follows:

1. Working with Water
2. Working with Stones
3. Working with Allies and Co-Walkers
4. Working with Plants and Herbs
5. Working with Living Creatures (animals, birds, fishes, insects)
6. Working with Touch or "Stroking": using the hands, or sometimes one hand or a specific finger. Usually the palms of the hands or fingertips.
7. Working with Signatures (which are powerful patterns in the surrounding environment)

There is no order of merit or superiority in our list, and it is not a checklist for acquiring skills or abilities. The Seven Aptitudes are simply inherent abilities that may be awakened through intent, through Faery or UnderWorld initiation, through practice, or as sometimes happens, spontaneously.

A Faery healer may use one or more of the Aptitudes, sometimes in sequence, sometimes working together simultaneously. Thus, in folkloric tradition, working with both water and stones often go together, in various permutations. In a greater sense, water is the universal medium of subtle energies, so we could say that working with water permeates all Seven Aptitudes in an infinite number of ways. As the Faery tradition is defined by its association with Faery beings, we could also say that the Aptitude for working with Allies and Co-Walkers is found in every branch of Faery Healing to a greater or lesser degree. So, do not take the Aptitudes as a literal checklist, but more as a starting point to help you discover and develop your potentials. In practice, there are always two or more Aptitudes interacting when we work on Faery Healing.

FINDING YOUR APTITUDES

Before working with one or more of the Aptitudes, we have to discover which of the Seven is best suited to us as individuals. This is often not a matter of choice or preference or even of inspiration. Poetically we might say that the Aptitudes choose us, rather than that we choose or discover or learn them. This same spiritual law applies to working with companion creatures, for it is the living creatures that choose us as partners and allies, and we do not select them.

One of the more difficult tasks for a contemporary man or woman wishing to develop skills in Faery Healing is that of finding, or being found by, their Aptitudes. The Aptitudes are inherent, usually more or less dormant within us. How can we find and awaken them? The methods described next are based on personal experience, as well as from practical group work over several years.

In working with groups of people, I have developed a simple visionary method which anyone can follow, preferably working outdoors. This outdoors working seems essential for finding the Aptitudes: if you live in a busy city you should try to work in a garden or park. Once you have found your basic Aptitude(s) you can then work anywhere, indoors or out.

Note: The following methods are enhanced by working with the recorded visions on the CD that accompanies this book.

Meditation One: Finding the Aptitudes I (working alone)

1. Find a quiet outdoor place.
2. Spend some time in silent meditation, becoming still.
3. Attune to the Four Elements, Above, and Below, then return to stillness at the center of the Seven Directions.
4. Let your Aptitude surface from deep within you. Do not choose anything; let it come spontaneously into the stillness.
5. When you are ready, return to outer awareness. Write some short notes on your experience.

This deceptively simple meditation may not work immediately or easily, so do not become impatient. Try the meditation regularly at the same time each day or night, but no more than once per day. Too much effort is always counterproductive with inner work.

Refining Meditation One: Finding the Aptitudes II
(working alone)

After some familiarity with our basic Meditation One, you might like to refine your method of working. As there are Seven Aptitudes, seek insights into one per day for seven days. Begin your meditation with a simple intention to meditate on the Aptitude for that day, but not with any forced or acquisitive desire to "get" that Aptitude, as this will close the very ability that you seek to open. Finding inner powers is like tightrope walking, a delicate balancing of consciousness will see you through to the other side, but no amount of intense concentration, will power, or determination can find that balance for you. Your self-motivation must be suspended in order to stay poised.

This refinement of our Meditation One may help with surfacing the Aptitudes, and will also allow many insights and inner awareness of the Aptitudes to develop. Make short notes after each meditation.

It is likely that some of the Aptitudes will be closed to you: do not let this worry you, there is plenty of work to be done within any one Aptitude, and each of them is sufficient for any healing work that you are called to do. If you persistently push towards Aptitudes that are naturally closed to you, you may experience a reduction of those that are easy, so be warned. In time, and with practice of other inner disciplines, you will be able to open out Aptitudes that were closed to you initially, should you need to do so.

HOW DO THE APTITUDES APPEAR?

The way in which the Aptitudes surface varies from person to person. They will make themselves known in simple individual work will be different to the way in which we experience their "surfacing" within group work. Some examples of group work will be discussed shortly.

In our intense workshops or experiential group sessions, no preliminary description is given of what might arise, so that we do not preempt or precondition the experience. In a book of this sort, the writer has the dilemma of how little or how much to say! The examples that I offer are not, therefore, a full list or a detailed guide for reference. They are merely examples from personal experience, and from many sessions working with others in groups.

1. *The Aptitudes may come to you as visions* during your silent meditation outdoors. In the most direct manner, you may have fleeting visions of water, stones, Co-Walkers or Allies, plants, animals, touching or stroking, and working with Signatures or patterns. In group work, we use this spontaneous vision idea within formal visualization. The individuals each have their own vision of Aptitudes while working within an overall guided scenario or visualization that is shared by the entire group, listening to the voice of the narrator.

2. *The Aptitudes may arise as physical sensations.* Often with Faery work, the body will generate physical sensations arising in response to subtle energies.

3. *The Aptitudes may come as Elemental intuitions.* You may have intuitions about one or more Aptitude. These will not come as intellectual or formulated concepts in words. They often arise as an affinity for, or deep sense of, Air, Fire, Water, Earth, Sky Above, or Land Below.

I have used this with good results in group work. A guided visualization based on the Elements, Sky, and UnderWorld, will often lead to spontaneous individual insights and intuitions about the Aptitudes.

4. *The Aptitudes may become apparent in dreams.* If meditations on the Aptitudes do not produce obvious or early "results," you may find hints in your dreams. Remember that dream work in the

Faery and UnderWorld traditions is not psychological. In the older traditions, rather than in materialist therapy, dreams are either taken literally or are "read" according to interpretive material from within the traditions themselves.

You will probably find it helpful to follow the widely used recommendation of keeping a simple dream journal. Ruthlessly ignore dreams that are not relevant: you will recognize Faery and UnderWorld dreams by their intensity and by the quality of Light (Earth Light), which often illuminates them. You may also find that you come to experience a combination of waking meditational insights and intense dream experiences about the Aptitudes.

5. *The Aptitudes may be revealed to you or within you by an Ally, Cousin, or Co-Walker*. This often occurs in meditations, dreams, and visions. Faery contact also comes suddenly in everyday circumstances; so do not assume that you must be in some altered state for a Cousin to reveal Aptitudes to you. As with *all* spiritual contacts, use your discretion and common sense, and do not let yourself be pixie-led by your own fantasies or wishful thinking.

6. *The Aptitudes may present themselves to you in the natural world*. This is the most traditional and reliable presentation. One or more Aptitude will come to you through the environment (this is why a goodly amount of outdoor work is essential for discovering your Aptitudes). How will they come? In very direct and literal ways: it may pour with rain upon you, you may trip over a stone, you may sense unseen presences, certain birds, animals or insects may come to you, your hands may burn or itch to touch something, or you may feel an intense communion with the shifting patterns of light, of air, of clouds, in the zone immediately around you. This list is a typical set of manifestations of all Seven Aptitudes, but there are many, many other possible manifestations of each Aptitude, as you will discover.

Do not allow sentiment or wishful thinking to trick you into making false identifications. An expression or manifestation of the Aptitudes is always accompanied by an enhanced awareness, a heightening of the vital energies, a shift of perception. It is not merely a synchronistic or coincidental event.

Meditation Two: Finding Aptitudes through Roadlessness

The physical presentation of Aptitudes, coming to you from the land or zone around you, is made more likely by a combination of stillness and walking meditation. There is a paradox and a mystery in this, for the Aptitude within you comes to you from the living land, and not through self -absorption or personal introspection and self- analysis.

1. Begin with stillness and the Directions (as described in Meditation One),
2. Allow yourself to walk and meet the Aptitudes, or for them to walk with you. Then return to stillness.
3. With practice, it is possible to merge walking meditation with inner stillness. This is the art known as "roadlessness" in Celtic tradition, while each of the older spiritual traditions has its own version: the Australian Aboriginal walkabout, the Native American vision-quest, and so forth.
4. You may find that certain Allies or Cousins are connected to specific Aptitudes. This connection between Faery beings and "supernatural" powers (which are, in truth, simply natural powers that we have denied) is exemplified in many folktales.

Let us briefly consider each of the Aptitudes in turn. In this chapter, we will examine the simplest basic attributes and methods of each Aptitude. Then, in Chapter 4, we will look at deeper and more interactive or advanced methods. In later chapters, we will consider the spiritual and planetary correlation of the Seven Aptitudes of Faery Healing, through the *Mystery of the Double Rose*.

WORKING WITH WATER

This is one of the most widely described methods of Faery and spirit healing. Water is used in various ways, and (as mentioned above) plays a mediating role in many of the other Aptitudes. Remember that the Elements interconnect with one another, and that each Element has something of the other three within it. Water, of course, is present in all body fluids and in all life forms to a greater or lesser degree, so it is of vital importance in any healing process. Traditionally, water is used in several ways for Faery Healing.

A bowl of spring water (ideally from the location in which you are working, though tap water will work if needed) is often charged or empowered by breathing upon it. This may be used to bathe an afflicted area, to drink, or for placing in a room for purification.

If you are fortunate you can use water from a healing spring, but be cautious with this, as such springs have unique telluric powers and inner Faery or spirit contacts. Because a spring is known to be therapeutic for traditional or other reasons, does not always imply that it is suitable for all uses. In traditional cultures, the powers of different springs were handed down in folklore and wisdom teachings. Today our task is more difficult, as we have to learn anew how to work with sacred or healing waters in a way that is apt and proper for the radically changed conditions of the 21st century.

In all examples of charging or empowering water, the charge is not permanent. Because water purifies and cleanses, bowls of charged water left in a room must be emptied away, ideally onto the earth or into a river or sea. Do not tip "used" water back into a spring. Water that is used for washing afflictions must also be disposed of carefully, as above. Water that someone drinks, of course, works its way through the body. You may use charged water for feeding plants, trees, stones, localities, and so forth, but you should not employ "used" water for watering plants.

These are the simple basics of the Aptitude for Water, but there is a great deal more in water working, and we shall return to it in the second part of this Summary.

WORKING WITH STONES

This is widely described in tradition, either in its own right or in connection with water. Typical examples from folklore include the power of standing stones or holed stones at ancient sites, sacred or blessed stones (usually small) used for healing, and the traditional method of letting affliction pass *into* a stone or stones (usually selected for this one-time purpose).

Working with stones falls into two simple categories: in the first, a curative, purifying or energizing power passes from the stone to the subject, and in the second, imbalanced subtle forces are passed from the subject into the stone. In the first category we find stones that have a timeless power within them – as far as we are concerned, it does not run out. We also find use of selected stones that are empowered or charged for a specific task. This may be for a one-time healing, or it may be for long-term use.

In the second category, the stone draws or receives unhealthy or imbalanced forces, drawing them from the subject. Usually the stone itself is then cleansed, often by placing it in running water. We will return to this import tradition of stones and water together shortly. The stone can also be buried, cast into a lake, river, or the ocean. Traditionally there are prayers or verses that are used to formulate intention and to seek the blessing of spiritual powers.

Stones in the first category may be "permanent" or "temporary." If they are permanent they are handed down, usually in families, or are especially empowered by ceremony. These are positive stones, and (without going into a pseudoscientific jargon) we might say that they have a beneficial agency or power vested in them long-term.

Stones in the second category are usually temporary. They are often picked up specifically for a task; sometimes they volunteer themselves in Roadless Meditation. More rarely, we will find or work with a stone that has a permanent quality of cleansing or drawing out of imbalance into itself. While the temporary stones are returned to the environment and cleansed by natural forces, the permanent stones of this type are retained and cleansed by special techniques, to be used again. Stones in this second category could be described as "neutral" or "passive" if they are temporary, and might be though of as "catabolic" or "negative" if they are used more permanently. By negative, we do not imply bad, but more in the sense of polarity, for they have a drawing or taking polarity that is used beneficially.

We can summarize the basic use of Stones as follows:

1. Permanent large stones located in one place may have powers that can be worked with. These may be natural or artifacts.

2. Permanent or enduring smaller stones (moveable) with positive/outgoing/giving curative or other powers.

3. Permanent smaller stones with negative/in-drawing/taking or cleansing powers

4. Temporary use of smaller stones in a variety of ways, positive/negative or giving/taking. This last group is the largest and most widespread use of stones in Faery Healing.

None of this short description is intended to be in any way scientific or definitive, and merely indicates some of the basics found in tradition, through contemporary use, and personal experience. I feel very strongly that we must not turn the arts of spiritual dynamics, such as Faery Healing, into some kind of false science. This was the major mistake of 19th Century occultism, while the major error of 20th Century occultism and New Age spiritualism has been to add false psychology to the false science.

WORKING WITH ALLIES AND CO-WALKERS

This is a major branch of the Faery and UnderWorld tradition, and of all primal and folkloric spiritual and magical arts. I have used the words *Allies* and *Co-Walkers* as these appear in Scottish Faery tradition at least as early as the 17th Century and so are not from modern concepts or books on neo-shamanism. Another old term used in Britain and Europe is *Cousins*, and we will use all three terms equally, as they have similar meaning. A more precise definition of each word can be made, but is not necessary for our general discussion of Faery Healing and related arts.

Our work with Cousins and Co-Walkers permeates all aspects of the Faery tradition, so much so that there is no tradition without it.

This may seem like an obvious statement, but the core definition of Faery Healing is that the healing takes place due to association and conscious intentional work with Faery beings. This is what makes it distinct from other types of spiritual healing.

Our first level of definition and description for each of the Seven Aptitudes is the simplest: *working with Cousins or Allies means that they take an active cooperative part in the healing process.* This cooperation may manifest in many different forms, and may be understood or explained by the healer in a wide variety of ways. At this basic level of description we will examine the relationship between human and Faery, and will discuss the more complex techniques later. We should remember that we are primarily exploring Aptitudes, so this section will not go further into the relationship between human and Faery beings.

If you have an Aptitude for healing with Cousins, this will be the way your healing work expresses itself to you most clearly. In some instances, the healer has a clear sense of relationship and identity of the Cousins, while in others he or she is only vaguely aware of their presence and cooperation. The basic rule of this way of working is that the Faery Co-Walkers usually work *through* a medium of manifestation. This medium can be water, stone, plants, and so forth, but is primarily the physical body of the healer.

Do not, under any circumstances, confuse this idea with spiritualist mediumship or New Age channeling. Let your work remain strictly within the Faery and UnderWorld tradition: there are similar ideas in all spiritual traditions, ancient or modern, genuine, or fake. If we focus on the practical aspects of the work, and attune strongly to the Faery tradition, all discussion and comparison becomes irrelevant. Remember that it is the attuning to the Faery level of consciousness and energy, and the use of tradition as a foundation, that enables Faery Healing.

The healer and the Allies work closely together: there are things that they can do that we cannot, likewise there are things that we can do that they cannot. Teamwork is the essence of this aspect of Faery Healing. The healer's body is present in the outer world, the surface world of nature; the Faery ally has a body in the inner world or deeper subtle realm of nature. Placing these bodies in close relationship triggers a powerful exchange of forces. In other branches of the tradition this exchange is used to trigger a range of transformations and experiences by humans, and eventually leads towards the Threefold Alliance of human, Faery, and creature which becomes a complete and fully functioning planetary being.

In Faery Healing, the exchange of energies is used to bring benefit, rebalance, and wholeness to the subject. This subject may be a human, animal, plant, or a seemingly inanimate entity such as a stone, an artifact, or location. In the Faery tradition, all things are alive and conscious, and there is no inert matter.

Traditional Ways of Working with Cousins

The traditional methods may be briefly described as follows (though this is not an exhaustive list or a guideline, it is merely a set of typical examples):

1. The Cousin works through and with the healer to empower water in various ways.
2. The Cousin works through and with the healer to empower stones in various ways.
3. The Cousin works directly with and through the healer, using his or her physical body as a medium or outlet source, to affect a cure or change in a subject. A wide range of techniques and vehicles or forms is found here: voice, touch (usually as in Aptitude 6), vision and use of the eyes, distance healing through contact and knowledge vested in the healer, ceremony, and so forth.
4. The Cousin works through and with the healer to select, empower, and prepare plants or herbs for healing work.
5. The Cousin works with the healer, with and through his or her relationship to other living creatures (a threefold alliance to bring healing).
6. The Cousin works with the healer, specifically through the hands.
7. The Cousin reveals the inherent power of Signatures or patterns to the healer, and helps to mediate this power through the healer to the subject.

WORKING WITH PLANTS

This Aptitude includes all plants: trees, flowers, herbs, mosses, and so forth. Before we explore this Aptitude, we should be clear on *what it is not*. In traditional Faery Healing, from folkloric magic handed down through the generations, the Aptitude for Faery Healing with plants is not herbal healing lore. This is very important to grasp from the outset: a person may be a good gardener; many have knowledge of healing herbs, may even be an herbal healer or naturopathic doctor. This does not inevitably mean that he or she has an Aptitude for Faery Healing with plants. Such an Aptitude may be present, or it may not be present: the answer is discovered through Faery attunement and practice, by using the methods of discovery (such as those in this book) that reveal your Aptitudes. As with many aspects of Faery tradition, your Aptitudes may take you by surprise!

The old herbal and plant healers were usually not Faery healers: they worked with the curative substances of the plants, according to an ancient healing tradition. The same applies today – herbal healing is not necessarily Faery Healing. If you are well versed in herbal healing, you still have to find your Aptitude for Faery Healing. This may or may not be one for working with plants in the Faery mode, consciousness, and energy. Contemporary people find this idea especially hard to grasp, but it comes clear in practice, much more so than through reading any explanation or text.

In herbal medicine, the gross substance of the plant is used. It is prepared and ingested or applied topically in various ways. In Faery Healing the healer works with the spiritual forces of the plant, and with certain Allies, Cousins, and Co-Walkers who are associated with specific plants or trees, or with the greater group entity of the entire species of a plant. In Faery Healing the plants are not cut, prepared, or ingested in any way. *It is the subtle forces of the plant allies that are used, not the substance.*

A good example of this is found in flower essence practices: there is nothing of the original plant substance in the essence, for it is a resonance imparted to the most sensitive medium of our world, the

Element of Water. The more it is diluted, the stronger it becomes. Flower essences are a modern development of the long established and well described traditions in Faery Healing, such as those of using the dew or condensed moisture from the surfaces of plants, flowers, and leaves for magical or healing purposes. The plant was never cut, for this would be to bring death. Healing can, and does come through death, of course. But the Faery tradition uses forces and directions of consciousness that are different from our human awareness, hence the seemingly miraculous nature of many cures reported in tradition.

We might say that the Aptitude for working with plants is really an aptitude for working with plant consciousness and energy. As in homoeopathy, where the potentized substance often works in a different way to the gross substance, working with plants does not always match up with the standard herbal effects used med-icinally. Indeed, the Faery healer who has a powerful plant ally can use this connection for any healing purpose, and it is not limited in the way the gross substance would be limited. Thus, a healer might have a strong alliance with the Oak Tree, and this is an actual and powerful Mystery explored later in this book. The Oak Tree alliance would be powerful for many forms of healing and trans-formation, most of which may be not be obviously connected to the gross or allopathic healing qualities found in the tree. What causes healing is the co-operation between the healer and the plant ally, not any herbal virtue or chemically traceable constituent in the plant itself.

Of course in practice, there are many connections, both obvious and subtle, between the nature of a plant and its use in Faery Healing, especially in essences and waters. But this cannot be forced into a rule-of-thumb checklist. One healer will have an affinity with the oak tree, or another tree or plant. Her abilities to work with this tree or plant are not necessarily connected to the standard definition that you would find in a popular flower essence book, in an herbal text, or in allopathic medical preparation and use. Another healer, working with the marigold flower, might obtain the same healing effects as the first healer using the oak forces, though his plant ally is very different.

This may seem, at first, confusing to the student, but it is resolved rapidly in practice. If you have an affinity for working with plants, build on it in meditation, vision, and practice. The plant allies will reveal themselves to you as and when they are needed. Usually you will have a small number of allies that are established long-term, and others will come to you in vision for particular tasks.

Working with plants will be strongly identified nowadays, by many readers, with the idea of flower essences, and this important association extends through the Aptitudes for working with water and with stones, to other essences and healing arts. Always remember that we are working with *Faery Healing*, and that it is the subtle forces and the communion with the Faery allies that make it so. An outer form, such as an essence, many or may not have a Faery Healing resonance and contact within it. It is up to you to form this connection through your spiritual work with plants, stones, water, and essences. You cannot just buy a Faery Healing essence. Once you have some practice in the subtle forces of Faery Healing, you will know, by touch, if an essence (in a store, on the shelf, from someone else) has Faery Healing power in it, or not. Your enhanced sense of touch, which arises from any and all of your Aptitudes, will also be useful in many other ways.

Flower Essences and Faery Tradition

This teaching could equally be placed in the Aptitude of Water, in the Aptitude of Touch, or in the Aptitude of Allies. It is placed here, in the Aptitude of Plants, as we have already touched on the differences between the gross substance, herbal healing, and working with plants in a spiritual manner, through the Faery Healing tradition.

Flower essences are directly derived from a frequently described aspect of the Faery tradition: the folkloric practice of using the dew or condensed natural moisture from flowers and plants. The classic example from folkloric practice in Britain is the gathering of dew from the grass and flowers on May morning (Beltinne or Beltain) to bath the face, or to look into, in a basin, and see future loves. Many variants of this custom are found in European traditional lore.

Modern flower essence practice originates with the British homeopath, Dr. Bach, who found that he could sense the potentials of certain plants and flowers, *by proximity*. This is significant for us, for the highly trained, sensitive homeopath was doing what Faery healers have done for centuries, attuning to the spiritual forces of plants. By being close to, or within the energetic field of, a tree or plant, we can discern the healing potentials that it holds and radiates. This is, in our description of Faery Healing, using one aspect of the Aptitude for working with Plants.

At this time, in the early 21st century, essences of all sorts abound, and not merely those of plants. They are nothing, more or less, than modern commercial variants of certain arts found within folkloric Faery tradition. They relate to the principles behind the Seven Aptitudes described elsewhere in this book. Thus, an essence made from a stone or a zone (Alaskan essences are a modern example) is a variant of the oft-reported method, from ancestral tradition, of pouring water over a sacred stone, and using the run off for healing purposes, or that of immersing a stone or a substance in a bowl of water, and using the water, but not the gross substance itself.

Flower essences, and the increasingly wide range of other essences, combine the spiritual properties of water with the spiritual proper-ties of other orders of life: plant, animal, mineral, atmospheric, solar, lunar, and so forth. Such combinations were widely found in the Faery Healing tradition. A healer might have an Aptitude for plants, or stones, or working with living creatures, combined with the Aptitude for working with water. Thus, healing waters were created.

The observant and thoughtful reader will have realized that there is one significant difference between traditional methods and those of the modern essence manufacturer: a difference of consciousness. The Faery healer has a conscious relationship with the living being and/or subtle energy that resonates into the water. Dr. Bach un-doubtedly had the same, though expressed through the world-view of homoeopathy. But many modern essences seem to be increasingly formulaic – do this, this, and this, and you have a workable essence.

There is no implied criticism or value judgment here, merely a statement of fact. The Faery healers had a conscious relationship with spiritual beings, a relationship that was embodied (according to their aptitudes) in a healing water or essence. Some flower essence practitioners unquestionably have a similar sensitivity to subtle forces, but it seems unlikely that it could be widespread in commercial use, as this precludes such connections, especially when essences are made in bulk and sold in stores.

The difference is in *consciousness and relationship*. The Faery healer works with inner contacts, allies, and a living relationship with spiritual forces that comes out through his or her Aptitudes. When essences or waters are prepared in this manner, they are highly focused and powerful. Such essences could not easily be distributed and sold commercially, as the healer has no connection to the user. However, healers may use pre-prepared essences, attune to the spiritual entities that resonate with such essences, and combine and administer them *consciously* as needed: to people, creatures, places, and so forth.

One very important aspect of using flowers is that they must be alive. The flower is the sexual organ and a major communicating organ of the plant. When flowers are cut to make essences, or the petals pulled, the essence is derived from a dying organ, not from the vitality and consciousness of the living plant.

In Chapter 5 on *Offerings,* we will discuss in detail that cut flowers are forbidden in the Faery tradition: to cut or pull flowers or to break branches as offerings is offensive. It is also aggressive. When you cut a flower, you kill it; when you break a branch, you kill it. Would you cut up the genitals of a beautiful loving man or woman because you wanted them to decorate your altar, and then watch them shrivel and dry up? Exactly!

Flowers and plants as offerings should be living plants to support and grace the altar – they are not consumed by anyone or anything. Thus you could choose plants in keeping with a theme or concept, and after they have been present for some time, they should be planted in the ground, if possible. From there, they will continue to work with the original intention and inner contact that you made when you placed them upon or around the altar. Strictly speaking, this use of flowers and plants is not an "offering," but more of a co-operation and attunement. The plants enhance the magic, but are not consumed.

WORKING WITH LIVING CREATURES

Something that might, at first glance, seem to be similar to this Aptitude has become widely popularized, and confused, through modern notions of neo-shamanism. Many people think, often at a very superficial level, that they know about animal allies: and a typical statement, often heard, written and published, is that animal allies must somehow embody qualities that the human would like to have. Typical examples of this attitude would be the strength of the lion, the swiftness and cunning of the fox, the flight of the eagle, and so forth. This psychological approach describes neither shamanic tradition, nor Faery tradition. It is, if we look beneath its potentially attractive surface presentation, nothing more than materialism masquerading as spirituality, with an utterly superficial human-centric focus of "what's in it for me." In both Faery tradition, and in ethnic shamanism, the living creature chooses you, whether you like it or not, whether you want it or not. So, when you work with the living creatures, the first step is to do away with any human-centric preconceptions.

Furthermore, when people who have practiced various modern neo-shamanic arts come to the Crossroads to find Companion Creatures, they are often surprised by what comes. Many people seem to use allies as props and comforts, and this attitude is subtly encouraged in many popular books and classes, though not of course, in true traditional ethnic shamanism. If you have an Aptitude for working with the living creatures, those that come to you at the Crossroads may not be those that you expect, or those that you have worked with in other contexts.

Traditional Aspects of Working with Creatures

In folkloric Faery practices, we find that living creatures play a direct and simple role. Faery dogs, for example, eat unhealthy matter or subtle forces (just, in nature, as dogs are scavengers). In myth and legend associated with Faery tradition, dogs are harbingers and carriers associated with death. Hounds will carry the soul to the otherworld, and Faery dogs warn of death, or assist with death.

Some spirit creatures exhibit surprising powers, very different from our modernist idea that animals, birds, fishes, and insects are somehow lower orders of life, less than humanity. Some spirit creatures act as powerful go-betweens that merge with, and mediate, the forces of other healing and transforming entities and energies. For example, insects often have a hive or collective consciousness that mediates healing forces; the bee is the best known example of this in both folklore and traditional medicine, but in Faery Healing it can be any insect collective.

As with plant allies, one or two powerful creature allies may enable a range of interactions through the human partner, and they are not always specific or limited to the traditional themes described above.

WORKING WITH TOUCH

This is, perhaps, the most superficial familiar area for the modern student. We all know, in some form or other, of healing that is transmitted by touch, or radiated through the hands. The most popular contemporary form at present is *reiki*, though there are many others. Healing with and through the hands has been with humanity for countless generations, and it may be that Faery Healing is one of the oldest forms. It is certainly enshrined in tradition, and well reported in historical examples.

Our first task, as modern individuals, is to disengage from what we already know (or think we know) about hands-on or energetic healing. Any previous knowledge or practice, or comparison in practice, will interfere with the subtle forces of Faery Healing. If you are working with your hands, do not try to force this skill into the mold of something else, but let it be uniquely itself. This is essential, as the Faery energies and consciousness work on their own frequency, and if we try to move into something else, we lose the contact. There are many spiritual and energetic forces that can and do flow through the body and are outlet through the hands, but most of them are not of the Faery realm.

Always go by the feeling: by what the Threefold Alliance or the Faery contact feels like. Certain spiritual healing forces will build up in your hands and arms, often giving a burning or electrical sensation. Learn to recognize this power, and do not cross-refer it to something, to anything, else.

The simplest method of working with hands is to commune with the Faery allies, or with any of the other Aptitudes and associated inner contacts, and feel their power merge through you. This merging triggers a specific energy, which flows out through your hands towards whatever subjects you may be working with. Sometimes this subject is a person, an animal, a tree, even a location. When you work in this manner the allies that work with you will often be on your right and left, and slightly behind you. The energies will build, be transmitted, and then fade when their work is done. Sometimes they will build and persist for a long period of time, so you have to learn how to stay with this.

In the deeper levels, a more complex teamwork pattern is built, which is described in the inner communication or received teaching on the *Double Rose* (Chapter 7). This involves your Threefold Alliance working through you; and beyond and behind the Alliance are the deeper powers of the Faery Go-Betweens and the larger spiritual beings that emerge from the Well of Light. They work, at a deeper level, through your allies. And the combined forces of all work through your Aptitude or aptitudes, often to outlet through the hands.

As a rule in Faery Healing, the hands are used to radiate or transmit, but some variants of the Aptitude imply that the hands are used to draw out and remove unhealthy forces. In this mode, the allies take the unhealthy forces, and remove them. This process will vary according to the kind of ally you work with: some will eat unhealthy matter, others will excise it, and some will carry it away in water or earth, and so forth.

WORKING WITH SIGNATURES

In some ways, this is the most obscure Aptitude, and it is perhaps the least commonly found. At the deepest levels of Faery magic, working with the composite of the White Rose, this Aptitude relates to the Mystery of the Seventh Companion who guards the Sleeping Maiden in the Forest. Although it is the rarest in practice, we have all experienced something of this Aptitude in our lives, for it involves intense memory.

A Signature is a moment of power in which many aspects of the natural and supernatural world merge together. A typical example would be a moment when you stand upon the cliff, the sun sets over the ocean, and a flight of geese flies overhead, heading south, calling out of the sky. The totality of this moment, in a concentrated form, is the Signature. Thus Signatures are held as key moments in our memory. They can only come spontaneously, and cannot be assembled or written up. Signatures always come outdoors, and usually take us by surprise.

The healer draws upon the totality of the Signature, which generates its special powers of time, place, and purpose. These complex forces flow through the healer: the Signature is a total energy source. There is some implication, in practice, that we can only hold a limited number of Signatures in our consciousness, possibly due to the typical memory phenomenon of conscious/ unconscious, remembered/forgotten, but more likely to be due to the sheer intensity of any Signature. More simply, we can only store so many before we are overloaded.

In practice, two or three powerful Signatures can last you a long time – some Signatures even endure between lives, and are recapitulated in meditation and at the Crossroads. Thus, we may find memories of Signatures that do not correlate to current life experiences, yet we remember them nevertheless. However, the main body of Signatures comes from this life, and not from the past. This is important to grasp, as much of the Signature energy flows through the body, so the presence of the body at the time of the original Signature is of great significance to the memory and recapturing and mediation of the Signature energies.

If you think about the nature of a Signature, such as the classic example described above, there are many forces and entities present. You can soon assemble a simple list: yourself, the geese, the sun, the sky, the land and sea, and the infinite other life forms all around you. Then add the spiritual presences such as your own allies, and the many other invisible beings of that place, power, and time. A Signature is like a symphony, but concentrated into one short intense moment.

Signatures and Sentiment

There is an understandable tendency for modern students to be sentimental about Signatures: "Surely that intense moment with my friend or lover, when we sat on the edge of the field of corn and poppies and look into one another's eyes must be a Signature?" Well, much as we would like it to be, it is not. Human sentiment or emotion, shared between humans, is not Signature energy. It has to be between a human or humans, spiritual entities, and the forces and forms of the planet, of nature. If we have a personal investment in the memory of the Signature, we lose the power. Signatures are impersonal or, perhaps more to the point, they are transpersonal. They are moments when we are uplifted from human concerns and human personal feelings, into a moment of communion with the living world and worlds all about us.

If you have an Aptitude for working with Signatures, you will probably want to spend time walking outdoors, preferably in remote places. All of the other Aptitudes can be found indoors through inner contact such as meeting at the Crossroads, though it must be said that Faery magic is much preferable outdoors. But Signatures are found in the living world of nature, not in a lounge. Some Signatures may speak of the subtle forces of the city, but they are usually of primal and undisturbed natural forces. The reasons for this should be obvious to us all.

FINDING YOUR APTITUDES,
USING THE RECORDED VISION ON THE CD

Now we have explored each of the Seven Aptitudes briefly, and found some simple and direct forms and visions for opening out your Aptitudes. At this stage you will find further material, especially with empowered contacts, on the CD that accompanies this book. Work with the CD after you have undertaken the basic forms described above. Your Aptitudes will open out considerably if you work in the order listed above, and then move on as follows:

1. The Crossroads Form (from the CD)
2. Finding Your Aptitudes (from the CD)

Here is the text for the empowered vision or *form* on the CD.

Finding Your Aptitudes

There are Seven Aptitudes in Faery Healing: everyone has at least one or more inherent within them. Sometimes your Aptitudes will surface spontaneously, but they are best worked with consciously, intentionally.

This form, Finding Your Aptitudes, will help to open out those inherent within you.

The Seven Aptitudes are:
• Working with Stones
• Working with Water

- Working with Plants
- Working with Living Creatures
- Working with Faery Allies
- Working with Touch
- Working with Signatures

The most powerful and rare is the Seventh Aptitude, working with Signatures, with includes, subtly, all the others. The Mystery of the Seventh Aptitude is linked to that of the Seventh Companion.

So let us proceed to the Crossroads, to discover our Aptitudes for Faery Healing.

Find yourself at the Crossroads, where the Four Hidden Ways come together.

Be aware of the Four Directions of East, South, North, and West.

In the East be aware of the Grassy Plains; in the South be aware of the White Hill; in the North be aware of the Sacred Mountain and dark forests; and in the West be aware of the mighty Ocean.

A stream flows out of the ocean of the West, from the ocean to the land, passing along the hidden way, to the centre of the Crossroads. From the centre it flows out to the East to water the grassy plains.

In the East the wind rises, and you breathe in deeply. Be aware of those mighty beings of the east that come weaving the whirlwind in their fingers: they draw close and their vigor fills your lungs.

In the South the White Hill utters light, and tall beings of opalescent flame descend the hill and draw close; their radiance fills your blood.

In the North the mighty ones of the mountains extend their presence and draw close; their strength fills your bones.

In the West the vast powers of ocean extend their presence along the hidden stream; their potency flows through the water in every cell of your body.

Form a clear intention in your mind that you will seek out your aptitudes, here and now, and in future dream vision and meditation.

(Music, then silence)

Be aware that you have passed down the Four Hidden Ways and discovered your Aptitudes. Be aware of the mighty Beings of East, South, North, and West whose power flows through your breath, your blood, your bones, and your flesh.

Come back to the Crossroads, and meet again with your Allies, Cousins, and Co-Walkers.

(Wild music here)

Here at the Crossroads form your intention to return to the human world, to redeem the surface world and bring it closer to the true and primal world. Open to the Sky Above, the Land Below, and the Four Directions of the land.

Now the Host at the Crossroads fades. You now come more fully into the human surface world.

Hold to your memory of what happened, and know your Aptitudes for Faery Healing.

With us is the Grace of the Shining Ones in the Mystery of Earth Light. Peace to all Signs and Shadows, Radiant Light to all Ways of Darkness, and the Living One of Light, Secret Unknown, Forever.

In our next Chapter, we will go deeper into the Aptitudes, using those of Stones and Water as models. Many of the methods, concepts, and inner teachings will apply to all of the Aptitudes, so this chapter rounds out the summary of Aptitudes, and includes further practical work for your development in the art of Faery Healing.

4. Deeper into the Aptitudes

In this chapter we go deeper into the Aptitudes, and use working with Stones and Water as our first examples or models. Much of this chapter will apply to all of the Aptitudes, so whatever are your Aptitudes or interests in Faery Healing, the information found here will be helpful.

There is a long and complex tradition of healing with stones in folkloric and Faery magic, and it demonstrates many of the concepts and methods that run through the entire Faery tradition, and many of the ways in which all Seven Aptitudes work for us, within us, and for others. Before we proceed to practical work in this healing art of Faery magic, we should briefly explore the historical ancestral context. Without context, information alone has little value. In Faery Healing, the tradition is the context, and the individual methods, and members of the Mystery, are the content.

THE RELATIONSHIP BETWEEN CONTEXT AND CONTENT

In a broader sense, the relationship between the spiritual world of the Faery allies and companion creatures, and us as humans and ancestors, is the overall context. This context is focused into specific traditional arts, often by ethnic or geographical areas, with overall continuity and connection across all the various areas or traditional arts. The content is, in the most immediate sense, our working team (as far as we are concerned) and thereafter it is found within the expanding network of holisms of the Threefold Alliance that contain the team, until the expansion of content includes the entire planet.

At that point, where it would seem that content and context become one, we all emerge into the greater context of the Solar World. The original content and context of the Earth and Lunar world are merged as one, within the consciousness and energy (context) of the Solar World. This in turn becomes united, solar context and content, within the universal context of the Stellar World. But, for practical purposes we focus on the world in which we live, the world of planet Earth, within the sphere of influence of the Moon, or as it is called in the Faery tradition, under the Moonlight.

Stones In Folkloric Healing

In a very simple sense there are two categories of healing with stones: large stones and small stones. The large stone workings are often associated with sacred sites, such as stone circles, dolmens, or standing stones, and in some examples, stones-of-power that have been placed by nature rather than by the ancestors. Small stone workings are often associated with a hereditary (though not necessarily familial) tradition of healing, whereby a healing stone or stones may be handed down through the generations.

A third group consists of stones that have come from, or been energetically charged by, stones from ancestral sites or from natural power places. These tend to be smaller stones, though sometimes larger pieces are found in a building or in a hidden location.

In large stone workings the two sub-categories are
1. Stones placed by ancestors
2. Stones placed by nature

The first group is associated with ancestral workshop sites or with stones that have come originally from ancestral sites. Typical traditions include those of passing someone's entire body through hole-stones or dolmen arches, touching or embracing a healing stone, or lying upon it or in its shadow. Sometimes the subject is asked to sleep on or beside a sacred stone.

In some folkloric healing traditions, water is poured over a large stone and subsequently used for healing. This combines the Aptitudes of working with Stones and Water and is, of course, eminently portable and practical. We come across this combination of Aptitudes often in Faery Healing, as the Aptitudes are not rigid definitions of unchanging abilities, but a flexible cycle or interactive range of psycho- spiritual potentials.

Small stones were traditionally kept wrapped in cloth. When we say "small" we mean easily portable, ranging in size from a pebble to a good-sized rock that can be carried without difficulty; anything bigger than that would be too heavy to move easily. Remember that the Faery tradition is "stuff free," and minimal. Anyone lugging bags of stones or large heavy rocks has completely missed the point, and is out of tune with the tradition. Light, portable, invisible: these are the key words.

Sometimes the wrapping-cloth itself was used in the healing process, by virtue of having wrapped and touched the stone. The cloth is laid upon the subject for healing, imparts its virtue, and is returned to the stone.

In folkloric methods in general, the stones (large or small) tend to work in one of two modes: anabolic (building) and catabolic (cleansing). Thus the cloth or water methods described, may energize the subject or may remove unhealthy forces from the subject. Traditional healers tended to work on the removal of influences and disease as their primary task. Very often that was the sole intention, and the subject's vital forces do the rest, in the natural process of recovery.

Some more sophisticated healers would practice a twofold method of both removing ill and giving forth benefit. This requires different Aptitudes to work together, or different modalities (catabolic, then anabolic) of one main Aptitude.

In most cases it was, and is, a matter of tradition and innate talent. To give a classic example, some traditional healers would only heal bleeding wounds through the use of a charged cloth. The cloth might be charged upon a stone, by the use of well water, or through laying on of hands with a prayer or charm muttering. Such healers stayed within their limits and could do nothing else. This is simply because they relied on innate Aptitudes and a received traditional method. Others, to continue with traditional examples, would only reduce fevers through water from standing stones. This second example also expands into a broader tradition, whereby people in general used water from sacred stones to cure ills, but were not, of themselves, Faery healers.

Relationship Between Aptitudes and Elements

In a traditional metaphysical sense, the stone is the element of Earth. Likewise cloth or fabric, though derived from a plant, is also the Element of Earth. Water, however, is not. Aptitudes have a tendency towards certain Elements (such as stones being of the element of Earth) but cross the Elemental distinctions. Thus someone with an Aptitude for working with Stones could work with Stones and Water, Stones and Fire, Stones and Air/breath, Stones and Earth or clay.

Thus each Aptitude may have a tendency towards an Element, but can be empowered by, and work with all four Elements acting in relationship to the core Context of the Aptitude. The Aptitude is the context; the Elements employed are the content or forces of the healing act. Next, we have a further context of all four Elements within which the healing takes place. This generates one of the typical threefold Faery tradition glyphs, of three concentric circles or spheres (figure 1).

Working with Stones today

In most cases today, we work with smaller stones. Those who are able to work with sacred stones at ancient sites or power stones in the landscape (if you live close by) should be extremely cautious and respectful in their choice of stones. At the end of this chapter we will offer some guidelines for choosing and building a relationship with larger stones, both at sacred sites and in natural power places. You should follow these guidelines very carefully if you intend to work with large stones. Why so? Easy to answer: we no longer live within the traditional context of our ancestral cultures, which formed long-term relationships with sacred stones over lifetimes, generations, and millenniums. If you cannot form a long-term day by day relationship with sacred stones or ancestral power places, you should be very cautious about beginning the long process of working with them. Reasons for this will become clear as we progress through this section on Healing with Stones.

FINDING STONES

In the old days, healing stones were handed down, either through a family or, as seems to have been more often the case, from one healer to a chosen heir. In many examples the healing stones were associated with a location, such as a spring or well, or even a house, and were not to be taken from them. Other stones, however, could be carried freely from place to place.

For the most part, this tradition has been broken. If you find someone claiming to be part of such a tradition, they are usually fantasizing. The test for membership of the old healing traditions is that the healer has no conscious description of the tradition and makes no claims. Indeed, in the Faery tradition, the old fashioned healers would never talk about what they did or how they did it. Making claims to being "in a family tradition" is a modern trait, and if it is genuine, refers to a modern line of teaching or set of practices. We could accept, of course, that someone learned certain things from a family member of the older generation, especially as we are now into the third generation of the occult spiritual and magical revival that began in the late 19th Century and gained huge impetus in the late 20th Century.

Older ancestral folkloric tradition taught that healing stones could be found or, more accurately, that *the stones find you*. This last includes, of course, the hereditary tradition, for the stones indicate to the healer where they wish to go, or whom they wish to work with after the healer's death. So the idea of us finding stones, or stones finding us, is eminently workable for the modern practitioner of Faery magic, and is one of the greatest assets and easiest practices for us all.

Furthermore this quality of *they find you* applies to all of the Aptitudes and Allies, so the general patterns described next will work with minimal changes for plants, living creatures, Faery allies, and Signatures. They all *find us*: we do not create them, summon them, or choose them.

Finding Your Stone

First note the heading: *Finding Your Stone*, singular. While you may eventually work with more that one stone, to begin with you need only one. If you cannot work with one stone, a set of stones will not improve your abilities. If you can work with one stone, you may not need any more.

As mentioned above, the stone finds you, no matter how much we think we are finding the stone.

Here are some typical methods that assist the Stone that is looking for you, always assuming that you have first established that Working with Stones is indeed your Aptitude. For having discovered the Aptitude, as described earlier, your shift of consciousness and your presence at the Crossroads alerts certain Allies and certain Stones. In a pseudo-technical sense, your change of energy/consciousness resonates with that of the Allies and the Stones. In a metaphysical sense, you and they all come together into a mutual world of consensual being. Prior to your discovery and opening out of your Aptitude, you were not in tune with one another and the connection was dormant. After going to the Crossroads, you becoming increasingly in tune with the Allies, Co-Workers, and

Elements of your Aptitude, and the connection is active. This applies to all of the Aptitudes, of course, not solely to working with Stones.

Dream Learning

On going to sleep each night, go to the Crossroads. Declare your intention to work in your sleep with your Aptitude (in this case for healing with stones), and invite your allies to work with you. This usually results in active and highly empowered dreams, though not always. In dramatic examples, people dream where they will find a healing stone. In most cases, though, the dream work helps to create the conditions whereby the stone finds you, often through one of the other methods described herein.

Walking learning

Here we make a differentiation between ordinary walking and Walking. The second type is *walking while within the Threefold Alliance*. From this point on we will call this Walking or Walking While Within. Here is how it is done:

1. Be still, and become aware of your Faery ally on one side and a spiritual creature on the other, to your right and left. (For this to work well, you should have already done the Crossroads exercises described in this book.)

2. Gradually you merge with the Allies, so that they are somewhat within you to the right and left side, and you are somewhat within them. This merged consciousness is the most simple and direct form of the Threefold Alliance. There are other deeper forms, but they tend to preclude physical movement. In this practice, we want to Walk.

3. Begin Walking. You can do this discovery process anywhere, with the obvious proviso that it has to be somewhere where you might discover a stone that you can carry. Ideal locations are the beach, the mountains, or the woods, but you can do this in the heart

of the city with equal effect.

4. As you Walk, things will look, feel, and even smell different, due to your being within the Threefold Alliance. Be sure to focus on your intention, which is to meet with a healing stone. Intense concentration is counter-productive, but a simple and clear intent is helpful. There are many novel and curious experiences that come from Walking While Within, so we need to be clear on our aim, and not be distracted by other things.

5. A stone will make itself known to you. Traditionally, this is called "twinkling." It is as if the stone, maybe lying with thousands of others on the beach, suddenly flashes a bolt of light at you. Another interesting and rather dramatic way of coming to the stone is that you are impelled to walk very fast or run a short way, and suddenly stop. The stone will be at your feet, or close by. Yet, another way is that you are walking at a steady pace, and you suddenly stop, knowing that the stone is near. In many examples, you will simply see the stone as you walk, and know that this is the one.

There are some simple rules to this art of being found by a healing stone.

1. It is always the first stone that commands attention. It may not be pretty or distinctive, though they often are. Do not change your mind, or spend hours selecting stones because you are not sure, want a better color, prefer a certain shape, and so forth. This is not shopping for a stone, but being found by a healing stone. It is *always* the first stone.

2. Begin to relate to the stone immediately. Work with it as soon as you pick it up. Do not merely put it in a bag and take home for later. Commune with it through touch. That night, sleep with it under your pillow, though there will be nights when you do not need or wish to do this.

3. As soon as possible go to the Crossroads, holding the stone. Offer it up at the Crossroads, while in your Threefold Alliance. Other beings will come to work with you, which are not part of your Threefold Alliance. These are the specific healing Allies that work with the stone, and/or with your Aptitude for working with Stones.

At a later stage they may attune to your Alliance, or become part of it for the healing purposes, but not permanently.

4. As a matter of common sense, remember to come out of the Threefold Alliance when you wish to return to the outer human awareness. This is done by simply indicating your intention, and focusing on the sky above, the land below, and your surrounding human environment. The Threefold Alliance will fade, though often resonances from it will continue for some time afterwards.

THE FOUR STAGES OF APTITUDE

1. Find your Aptitude
2. Find your Allies (in that Aptitude)
3. Work within (yourself in the Aptitude, with the Allies)
4. Work without (outside yourself, but in the Aptitude, with the Allies)

So in our example, you have found your Aptitude for working with Stones.

Next, you find your Allies; first by letting the stone find you, then by going to the Crossroads with the stone to find further Allies. Allies, in this definition, are the stone, and the members of your Threefold Alliance (though this may change in healing magic) such as Faery beings or spiritual companion creatures that come to you at the Crossroads to support your Aptitude.

Notice that two of the Aptitudes (working with the Living Creatures, working with Faery Cousins) are inherent in all the others. Aptitudes are interactive, not static.

WORKING WITHIN THE STONE

The third phase is Working Within. This involves attuning, vision, and practice with the Aptitude. There are a number of helpful stone meditations, and you will find others as you go deeper into the art.

Basic Stone Meditation

1. Hold your stone, resting it gently in your cupped hands, relaxed. Feel it through your skin. Just feel it, do not strain or try to have visions or make contact mentally, just feel the stone.

2. Imagine the origin of the stone. Was it once part of a mountain? Did it come down with glacial ice? Was it rounded on the bed of an ancient ocean, rolled in a mighty river, cracked from frozen ice strata, thrown up in a volcanic eruption or earthquake? Just simply imagine the many origins of the stone, feeling its surface. Eventually the stone will reply.

3. When the stone replies, it may come through in some unusual manner, not necessarily with a story of its origins. The Origin Imagination is something for humans to attune through.

4. Be prepared for various kinds of Faery or spirit beings to come through the stone when it responds. Some of these may be large, others smaller. They will often come in a rush, so you have to be calm. Form a clear intention in your mind that you are concerned with Healing. Other offers may come from the Stone Allies, but at this time you are concerned with Healing.

5. Gradually you will feel the sensation of the stone change. As you begin to move deeper into communion with it, the dramatic (early) sense of the Allies fades. Sometimes the stone will grow noticeably hot, sometimes cold. It may also resonate or vibrate a high frequency of movement that you can just feel, like a tingling sensation. When any of these changes occur, the stone is ready for work.

6. For initial spiritual work, you may use the stone upon the zones of your own body, as shown in Figure 2. The main zones are the Feet, Loins, Heart, and Head. Sense and feel how the stone works with these zones in your own body.

7. Once you have your sense of (5) and (6) you can begin to call upon the Allies to work more powerfully through the stone. Do not do this before practicing stages (5) and (6), or you run the risk of either overloading yourself or, more usually, causing the Allies to back off because they sense that you have not practiced the art sufficiently.

How Allies Work Through Aptitudes

When the Allies work more powerfully through a stone, they follow the basic principles that apply to all Aptitudes:
1. Working through the chosen medium (Stone, Water, Plant, Creature, Touch, Faery Allies, and Signatures).
2. Working from behind you, through your body, or through your hands as they touch the stone.
3. Entering into Alliance on one or both sides of you. Sometimes they will join to your existing Allies, right and left, extending the Alliance. In the deeper and more practiced stages of the work, they may temporarily replace one or more of your basic Allies that comprise your usual Threefold Alliance.
4. More rarely, they will work directly upon the subject, while you and your Allies are working through the Aptitude (in this case, the healing stone).

WORKING WITHOUT

The simplest method is to place the stone upon the subject. You do not need to place it upon any source of pain or discomfort, even though this might seem the most effective way. Indeed, you will often be directed by the Allies to place it on some other zone altogether, to ask the subject to hold it, or place it touching or under the subject (remember that much of your healing will not be done with human subjects!).

Important note: if you are working on a human, including yourself, *do not* combine or confuse this method with some other technique or information shown on a chart of the subtle forces of the body, such as reflexology, chakra maps, acupuncture points, and so forth. If you do this, you will fail. Faery Healing takes no notice of human charts and theories, and if you try to cross-reference it to one of the many systems popular today, you are completely missing the point, the purpose, and the power of Faery Healing.

The body zones of Feet, Loins, Heart, and Head include all the various theoretical and practical meridians and energy centers, but Faery energies do not always follow these traditional healing or energetic patterns. Remember that the Crossroads is made from the Four Hidden Ways. The hidden ways of Faery Healing obviate time, space, and energy, as we understand them.

OTHER OCCURRENCES

With practice you will find that the Allies suggest a variety of methods to you. A healing stone might be put somewhere in the room, but not on the body of the subject. It might be buried in the garden, or under the threshold (i.e. somewhere where the subject walks over it while going to and fro, day by day). They may also suggest that the stone is held for a while by someone else, such as a family member, lover, or close friend.

The stone may be immersed in water, and the water used to bathe the head, feet, or hands of the subject. In these examples, we are following a human-centric model, but you may equally have to do this for an animal, fish, or bird.

Of course for a fish, you would immerse the stone in the water that the fish swims within, or add some charged water from the stone to the water that holds the fish. This is not limited, by the way, to a domestic fish tank, but can be done in rivers or seas where there are imbalances. Faery magic works extensively with water, and has a resonant homeopathic effect within all bodies of water.

WHEN THE WORK IS DONE

There are two main stages: cleansing and charging. The stone should be cleansed when the work is done. Do this regardless of any deep cleansing or withdrawing work done on the subject. The Allies may draw unhealthy forces away, but there is often a residue upon the stone. This will sometimes appear as a gray ash-like substance or, as many find, the stone feels sticky. The cleansing depends, again, upon your Aptitudes. Some healers will clean it with earth, and scatter the earth. Others will clean it with water, and scatter the water. More rarely you many clean it with salt, if it is truly grimy. Afterwards, clean it with fresh spring water to wash away salt traces.

Next the stone is laid to rest overnight: do not try to re-attune or charge it immediately. There are subtle processes that must work before we continue, and there is, poetically and magically, a time for the stone to "rest" – and for you to rest, also.

To charge the stone after cleansing and rest, simply go to the Crossroads and offer it up to the Allies. This is the simplest way to recharge it. Once a stone starts to build power, this is more of a formality or confirmation, but in the early stages it is part of the process of developing the innate power of the stone, and bringing it to maximum potential.

HEALING AND WORKING WITH WATER

Water is the most prominent element reported from tradition in Faery Healing. Healing with water is also, of course, known world wide in every folkloric and magical tradition. In many ways, your entire Faery Healing work involves water; as our bodies are mainly water, and the subtle forces of Faery Healing work through the body. But for that water, be it Within or Without, nothing would work.

As a helpful meditation, consider how water is present in all Seven Aptitudes, and how it relates to each Aptitude. You will be surprised at the wealth of connections and insights that arises when you do this!

Folkloric Water Healing

The most common techniques involve using a bowl of water, often with associated prayers, or muttered or whispered charms. Water is also used in association with stones, blessed objects, and washing rituals. In work with plant allies (the Aptitude of working with Plants) water is potentized by contact with the plant or flower. This is what is widely known today as essence therapy, a healing art that originated with the Faery tradition. Flower essences did not, as is popularly assumed and commonly reported, originate with Dr. Bach in Britain, though he formulated the method according to homeopathic principles and his own insights. Indeed, potentized essences have been used in the Faery tradition for many centuries; and traditional arts such as washing stones, drinking or bathing in morning dew, or taking drops of rain from flowers, are widely reported by commentators, folklorists, antiquarians, and so forth.

THE ELEMENT OF WATER

Faery Healing is not based on an Elemental system (as we might superficially suppose) but upon the interaction of three components; Elements, Entities, and the Aptitudes. To give a significant example, healing with water is not in any way dependant on working with Water Elementals, or those Faery beings that live in the streams, rivers, lakes, and seas. Indeed, many of the healing allies are those more typical fiery in nature, or earthy, but they work with us through water, providing we have an Aptitude for it.

The Element of Water permeates all existence in our world, and in many other worlds. It is this permeation and omnipresence that enables the healing work, for water is a sensitive medium through which energies or resonances can be transferred. The transference through water is astounding, for it can reach for many miles almost instantaneously. This is one of the "secrets" of the Faery Healing arts, and is closely related to the resonance principle described in homeopathy. The main difference being that the Faery tradition works consciously with spiritual Allies.

COMING AWAKE TO WATER

When we work with stones, the specific and individual healing stones find us. This is not so with water, for we are already within the vast ocean of living Water, both in our bodies, and in the land and air and sea within which we exist, without which we would cease to be.

Once you have gone to the Crossroads and discovered that you have an Aptitude for working with Water, you have to come awake to Water. Only after this has happened can you practice the healing arts and other aspects of Faery tradition that go with Water. In some circumstances, rare today, you may form an inner connection with a specific body of water, such as a well, spring, river, or lake. Usually such connections require living in one place, and may ultimately prove unsuitable for the modern human. As we are in a time of major transition, it is difficult to judge this, and you must make your decisions and live accordingly.

One method of coming into a more conscious relationship with Water is *Water and Breath*. This is a sacro-magical art found in many forms throughout human culture. In a cosmic sense, our breath upon water mirrors the process of creation. There are three levels to this action of breathing upon water:

1. The universal, in which the Breathe of Life utters itself out of the Void, and the creation of the cosmos begins;
2. The planetary, in which the great oceans of our world receive subtle forces from the moon, sun, and stars;
3. The human, in which we breathe upon water. *When we do so, our allies in Faery Healing breathe with us and often breathe through us.*

Usually, the water is a small body in a vessel, but in some circumstances it can be a river, or the ocean itself.

Ideally all three of the above should flow through you when you breathe, but if you can establish the communion of stage (3), that will be sufficient in the early stages of your work. Why is this so simple? Because moon, sun, and stars already breathe through us (see *The Miracle Tree*), and we are already within the universal Breath of Life.

5. Offerings

Offerings play an important role in folkloric magic, and are part of the practical tradition of the relationship between human and Faery races. If you are to build an ongoing relationship with Allies in your practice of Faery Healing, or of Faery magic in general, you should pay close attention to the practice of making offerings. It is an intensely effective magical form, but is often misrepresented and misunderstood. This chapter aims to clarify the idea of offerings and to establish some guidelines for good practice.

In the modern revival of paganism and witchcraft, the practice of offerings has been substantially reinstated in ceremonies, homes, and at ritual sites, including those ancient sites associated with ancestors, deities, and Faery tradition. Before we explore the philosophy and metaphysics behind the idea of offerings, let us consider some ground rules. Even in these ground rules, we will find, inevitably, some of the spiritual principles.

It is clear from witnessing offerings in both Europe and the United States, and from visiting both ancient sacred sites and modern ritual sites or shrines, that many modern people, no matter how dedicated or well intentioned, do not seem to know or even care about some of the basic rules and practices concerning offerings. Many private shrines or temples are, surprisingly, polluted by rotting offerings. Many sacred sites in Britain and Ireland are filthy with rotten decaying offerings, trash, candle wax, discarded clothing and other items left, presumably and sometimes certainly (as witnessed), by self-styled pagans who do not clean up after themselves. This is sacrilege – an offense against the deities, the ancestors, and the Faery contacts. Sadly, it is yet another manifestation of the human indifference to the sacred living land and sea, and truly one of the worst manifestations, right at the heart of the practices that should be dedicated to transforming and redeeming human indifference and selfishness. How can we expect to heal, to transform either the living world or ourselves when we do not live according to some of the basic rules of spiritual life?

THE BASIC RULES

The basic rules of offerings are simple and well established in traditional practice. Here is a contemporary checklist, broadly based on recorded evidence of tradition and ritual going back to the ancient world and of folkloric practices worldwide. The spiritual laws of offerings are not only enshrined in history and ancestral practice, but are the laws of courtesy, common sense, and basic hygiene.

1. *Offerings must be made in a clean, respectful manner.* A small offering with pure intent is more powerful than a pile of offerings idly cast down with a wish. Offerings should be placed on clean stones or surfaces, for example, and not thrown around carelessly. They are gifts for the deities, the ancestors, or the Faeries. Would you want your gifts of food and drink to be thrown in a heap in a dirty spot and then left to rot? The modern pagan should compare revival western pagan practices with those of, say, the Hindu temples of India, where all offerings are clean, harmoniously placed and arranged, and never left to decay on the altar or in the temple. This comparison is helpful because of the unbroken tradition of offerings in Hindu culture that goes back thousands of years. And, it need hardly be said, Hinduism is a pagan religion!

2. Offerings of food, drink, or anything that decays should only be left overnight. The next day they should be cleaned up and buried. The Faery tradition, following on the practices of the ancient world, asserts that the *essence* of the offering is absorbed

by the Faery allies, but not the gross *substance*. This is a very significant and valuable teaching found in traditional practices and described as early as 1692 by the Rev. Robert Kirk, in *The Secret Commonwealth of Elves, Fauns and Fairies*.

What remains after 24 hours must be buried to continue to decay naturally: it cannot be consumed, for it has no essence.

It is worth considering that, in the ancient world, anyone taking offerings for themselves was accursed; and the esoteric implication is that they consumed the dead substance of the offering, thereby cursing themselves. This tradition excludes, of course, those offerings that were shared in a communal meal, as in many rituals. But what we eat at that meal is clean, fresh, and vital. We do not leave it to rot on our shared table or altar.

Nor should an offering merely be left in a location away from the original altar or offering site, there to decay. For once it has crossed the threshold between life and death, it is no longer an active gift or offering, and now belongs to those forces of break-down and decay that work to regenerate the earth. Sometimes we hear or read that the biological decay of offerings at a sacred site is part of the offering process. There is nothing in tradition or in the tenets of the ancient world as handed down to us in literature that implies this; but there is everything about properly sanctified, purified, and energized offerings, and how a sacred place is kept strictly clean and harmoniously attuned. As is your altar, so is your heart and soul. And because the shrine, the circle, the altar, is a meeting place for many humans, Faery beings, spirits, allies, gods and goddesses, your heart and soul is on full display according to how you keep that sacred place and what you offer there.

Exceptions to this rule might be if the intention is to intentionally invoke forces of decay and disease, but this should not be undertaken lightly, and certainly it should never be undertaken in a place dedicated to forces of creation and balance. A healing shrine should not be filled with stale grease, decaying underwear, rancid perfumed oil, food wrappers, prayer notes under lumps of rotten cheese, melted chocolate, and fly covered stinking fruit (as I saw recently in the ancestral shrine of a sacred goddess well in Cornwall).

3. Bio-degradable offerings, of any sort, must not be left to rot on your outdoor altar, in a sacred place, or anywhere else. Would you like this to happen in your house? No? Then do not expect the deities, ancestors, or Faery allies to like it. While I have seen many rotten offerings outdoors, even in people's garden shrines, I have never seen any on altars in houses. (Though, we have all seen cluttered, untidy, confused, and even dusty altars, have we not?) Yet, no one who leaves offerings outside to decay, but cleans them off their indoor altar, seems to sense the paradox in this.

Bio-degradability has thresholds and has its proper place: within the earth or within the compost heap, not upon the altar or around the ancestral sacred site. This is a deeply spiritual law, which is exactly why it extends to the realm of hygiene in daily life. Each order of life, from the whale to the anaerobic bacterium, has its proper function and place.

4. Some offerings, such as drink poured upon the ground or into flowing water, are immediately absorbed. When you make these, ensure that they are not substances that will cause imbalance, such as heavily sugared drinks or perfumes. Heavy sugars or salts can do a surprising amount of damage, even in small quantities. Do you want your offering to poison and kill? Consider how the myriad life forms, of the animal, insect, and microscopic worlds, will react to your offering, and how it should benefit them according to your good will, love, and compassion.

5. Other offerings, of more solid items, such as metals, stones, artifacts, should be sunk deep in water or buried. They should not left to lie around to be misused or to clutter up a sacred site. Why do you think archaeologists and treasure hunters spend so much time digging? Not merely because people buried treasure to hide it, but because our ancestors' offerings were intentionally buried to enter the UnderWorld, or were cast reverently into deep pools and sacred springs, passing beyond the reach of humans.[1]

6. *Always clean up thoroughly after offerings and rituals.* If you arrive in a place and find that others have polluted it, be ready and willing to clean up before you make offerings. Many sites have multiple layers of offerings, prayer letters, tokens, and candle wax

piled upon one another and left stinking and foul. Do modern-day pagans, wiccans, and Faery practitioners really think that this is acceptable, either to one another or to the sacred powers and divine ones that they seek to contact?

7. Be thoughtful with your offerings. In some ways, they truly represent *what you are* to the spiritual worlds. So, consider well what you offer, how you offer it, and what you do with the offerings after they have been accepted.

USE OF CUT FLOWERS AND BRANCHES

It has become customary, possibly from Christian Church traditions, to use cut flowers, bunches of flowers, or cut flowering branches as offerings. This is highly offensive and insulting: the flower is not only the sexual organ of the plant, but is also its higher organ of spiritual communication. So, along come some humans who cut a bunch of flowers and offer them on an altar or, worse still, at an ancient sacred site. The dying organs of the plant that has been attacked and mutilated are then left to rot. Even if the flowers are in water, they are still dying, and are still the result of mutilation of the living plant.

Anyone with a fraction of spiritual sensitivity will realize how absurd, thoughtless, and utterly human-centric this practice is. It is such an accepted facet of daily life, in a non-magical context, that no one even thinks about it. If you want a good living relationship with the spiritual forces, especially with the Faery allies, creatures, and plants, now is indeed the time to think and change if you have been using cut flowers.

As a side note on cut flowers, I remember a spiritualist medium saying, years ago, that her "spirit guides" *fed off the energy* released by cut flowers, and that this was why flowers were always welcome in a séance or on an altar in a spiritualist church. I later discovered that this is widely taught and believed in spiritualist or channeling circles, and is regarded as normal practice by many. This statement about spiritual entities *feeding on the energies of dying flowers* raises many questions, but in the Faery context it is clearly inappropriate. Traditionally, Faeries are said to draw vital sustenance from the living joyous plants and flowers, but not from the mutilated and dying!

In the ballad of Tam Lin, Janet pulls roses to force Tam Lin to appear, and he expressly forbids her to "pull those flowers" or to "break those wands." Later in the same story, she threatens to pull another plant or "the scathing tree" (to scathe means to wound), which would abort her child. But we discover that her motives are not truly coercive, but born of desperation. There is an implication that this is the only way to bring her lover to the threshold of the human world. When we explore the Mystery of the Double Rose, (Chapter 7) we will discover how this motif relates to sexuality, fertility, and the redemption ritual by which Tam Lin is drawn back to the human world. This example of potentially coercive magic from a determined lover reveals the taboos or restrictions of the tradition in a number of ways.

Let us move on now to some of the magical and spiritual principles in the idea of offerings.

THE THEORY, PRINCIPLES, AND PRACTICES OF OFFERINGS

The basic theory behind offerings is simple: we give a gift to someone else. That someone can be a friend, a superior, a god or goddess, the spirit of a place, a Faery ally, or a spiritual companion creature. It can be a stone or a mountain, a flower or a tree, a well or a pool, or a river or an ocean. It can be anything, in other words, that is not obviously ourselves. Offerings are given to the *Other*, be it a lover, a deity, or the dancing stars in the night sky.

From that simple definition, many patterns, practices, and disputes have arisen. To the orthodox religions, offerings within folkloric tradition are, at best, superstition or evil ritual practices, at worst. To the anthropologist, psychologist, or academic researcher, offerings are the practices of the ignorant, of those who have not been enlightened by materialist science and the onrush of modernism. In some cases, such as revival pagans and wiccans, they are utterly modern people who have, for various reasons, chosen to indulge in ritualistic superstitious or atavistic practices, or so a psychologist might presume. But the concept of offerings, of gifts to the *Other*, is deeply rooted in the human consciousness, and it can be carried out with grace, love, and unconditional communion, if we so choose.

For many of those who give offerings, the idea is one of a trade: I will give X in return for my wish of Y. In some primal traditions, world-wide offerings are coerced and are made out of fear. Nor are the Christian churches exempt from a long history of coercion for profit, so we need not think that coercive offerings are exclusively "primitive" or "ignorant."

There are two kinds of magic: coercive and co-operative. Humans can be coerced by their beliefs and by one another, and they can also engage in coercive magic to gain temporary benefit. In our context of the Faery tradition, we use co-operative magic. Our not-so-distant ancestors also used co-operative magic, and it is this stream of co-operative magic that we should tap into. Let it be known that I am not saying that ancestors never used coercive magic – to think so would be naïve and romantic. But if we are to have a creative ongoing revival of magical paganism, that builds for the future and seeks to heal the wounded world, we should explore the co-operative magic of our revered forebears, drawing on the best, and then seeking to make it better and better suited to our times. Let us explore this idea further, by considering the metaphysical principles behind offerings.

THE PRINCIPLES OF OFFERING

1. Offerings are a way of sharing and of making relationships. When humans offered sweet baked cakes and honey wine to the Faery beings on the land, they were not trying to bribe them. Consider this: what is a cake? Is it just some highly sugared, brightly colored, semi-poisonous, nutrition-free item that you buy in a store? It might

be such today, but not so long ago it was made at home. And still should be, if you are serious about the spiritual principles of your offerings. And what is wine? Another store-bought item, laced with chemicals, coloring, sulfites, and traces of pesticide? Our cakes and wines for offerings should be the fruits of at least some of our labor, made with our hands, and intended for the ritual. The spirit allies, the gods and goddesses, will sense this and respond to your love and your labor.

Cakes are the manifest results of the labor undertaken and the grains that grew through the year. These are transformed into something unique to humans by the uniquely human baking process. The wine is fermented by human skills and comes from the fruits, the herbs, or the honey of the bees. Thus we are giving back the gifts of the land *transformed through human interaction*, and offering a share of this out of respect for those spirit beings that helped us grow the plants that made the foundational materials for the cakes and wine.

When we make such offerings, we are also saying that we are in a community with those beings of the spiritual world and are willing to share with them. They take, according to tradition, "the pith and essence" of the offerings, and leave the gross substance, which becomes inert. In modern terms, we might say that they take the vital energy but not the outer shell. The most humble homemade offering has more power in it than a gaudy item from a store.

2. Offerings, therefore, contain something uniquely human, which is given as a gift. They are not bribes, but ways of interacting and sharing. Traditionally, it is said that when offerings are maintained over a period of time, a good relationship builds up between the humans and the spirits. So offerings are also about long-term patterns, and not merely about desperation or propitiation in time of need.

3. Some offerings, however, are made appropriately while asking for help. This is enshrined in tradition, and is summed up in the phrase that is quoted in several places in this book: *There are things that They can do that We cannot, and there are things that We can do that They cannot.*

Offerings asking for help, protection, blessing, are not made out of fear. They are part of the co-operative magic outlined above, and ideally, should be part of a cycle of offerings as described in (1). Regrettably humans often only resort to offerings when they want something, or to avert an impending disaster – just like praying in orthodox religion.

If you make offerings, keep them going frequently, in a cycle of at least a year in the same place, and discover and observe the responses. You may be surprised!

4. Offerings are also given as gifts of thanks and out of respect. This aspect is important, for such offerings are not given with thought of return, but are given unconditionally as acknowledgement of the existence of the Faery beings, the living creatures, and the mysterious spiritual powers. We give our friends and loved ones gifts, because we appreciate them and want them to be happy. What could be better than that?

An Encounter with Ants

To close this stern chapter on Offerings, I would like to tell a short, amusing tale as an offering to the reader; something wonderful from my own experience. It involves offerings and how they sometimes work in practice.

A few years ago, I read a wonderful book by David Abrams, called *The Spell of the Sensuous*. In one part, the author describes how he saw offerings of rice being made in the Far East, and how the ants carried them off daily, but did not come into the open sided dwellings of the people. He concluded that a good relationship had been built between the humans and the ants that benefited both races by this simple practice of offerings. The ants had food daily, and the humans could prepare their own food in houses with no walls, without being annoyed by industrious ants coming in to forage and carry off whatever they could from the food area. This arrangement was what a business person would call a win-win situation, and all due to the ancient wisdom of making offerings and communing with other orders of life. The story demonstrated very well, not only the common sense application of offerings over a long period of time to establish patterns of mutual tolerance and life together, but also had many spiritual and magical implications.

The morning after reading this inspiring anecdote, as if by magical coincidence, I found many ants on the counter-top in my kitchen. They were the tiny ants that seem to get into anything and everything, and a steady parade was coming in through a minute hole over the sink. I knew, from experience, that blocking the hole would make no difference, as they would just reappear through another undiscovered access point. I had no intention of laying down poison, so I had to think of another way, as I did not want to have to be cleaning and killing each day until the parade stopped. So, thinking of what David Abrams had witnessed, I set out to find the ants' nest. Tracking back to the garden, I found that they were coming from a substantial entrance in the earth, and that there was obviously a large nest down there. So, I decided to make them an offering right there where they could find it each day, and to ask them to stay out of the kitchen.

The offering was made by pouring some honey just outside the entrance to the nest with a friendly request that they take this honey and stay out of my house; within a few minutes, many ants were carrying it away into the UnderWorld. Good, I thought, and we can do this everyday! I left sensing that my good will had been well received.

The next morning, I arose early, and found my counter-top completely free of ants. Not one was to be seen. It had worked! As the sun rose higher, I remembered that it was time to make the offering, and opened the cupboard to take out the honey jar, go outside, and pour. To my astonishment I found that the jar was covered in many layers of busy ants, like a black ball, all trying to get inside! I was dismayed, and then I laughed. They had come right to the source, to the place where the offering was kept, unerringly. After all, I had offered them the honey, and from that moment of offering, it was their honey and was no longer mine. For a brief instant I even wondered if they were trying to save me the trouble of going outside, but that would be a human rationalization, and I dismissed the thought.

So I took the entire jar, ants and all, outside near to the nest, shook the ants off, and opened it, leaving it open for them. Over a short period of time they emptied all the honey and they did not come into the kitchen again.

This delightful and happy sequence of events reminded me of many folk tales about humans and ants. From the time of our communion and their acceptance of my offering (all of it), I could have called upon help from those ants. Perhaps I have.

Notes:

1. See, for example, the famous hoard of offerings found at Llyn Cerrig Bach Lake on Anglesey, which archaeologists think were Druid offerings, sunk deep in the water.

6. The Forms and Visions of Faery Healing

In this chapter, there is a series of forms and empowered visions to assist you in your skills, to open out Inner Contact, to strengthen your Threefold Alliance, and to bring you deeper into the Mystery of the Double Rose. Some of these forms are found on the CD of visionary workings that comes with the book, while others are referred to in various chapters according to their context and practice in Faery Healing and Earth Healing.

We begin where everything begins and ends in Faery magic, and in all magic – at the Crossroads.

THE CROSSROADS FORM

Note: this form opens the CD, and is essential for your ongoing practice of Faery Healing and Faery magic. Work with it often, until you can do it from memory without the recording or the text.

This is the basic pattern for the Crossroads form. In practice it will often change according to your location. The Crossroads can be on the plains, in the mountains, by the seashore, in the desert, or in the middle of the big city; anywhere the Seven Directions and the Four Hidden Ways come together.

Coming Into the Directions

Begin by being still, stilling your sense of time and space, and ceasing all movement but for breath, in and out.

Be aware, first and last, of the Sky Above and the Land Below; and of the Directions of the Land, which are East, South, North, and West. So you have a Direction behind you, and a Direction before you, and to your right and to your left. The Direction behind you flows through you, and moves you forward. The Direction before you flows to you and creates according to your movement. Those on your right and left strengthen and uphold you.

Now you have a sense of place, of the center, of your true home which is neither here nor there, but at the heart of the Four Directions.

The Crossroads

Find yourself at the Crossroads, where the Four Hidden Ways come together. The Four Hidden Ways of the World, that make long journeys short, and short ways heavy with unimagined time. The Hidden Ways that pass through all places, all times, all events, secret and concealed, yet open and visible to all who have eyes to see and hearts to feel.

The Crossroads is an open place, with four plain simple track ways meeting in the center. They come, all four, to the central stone, which is a small upright stone carved with spiral patterns.

The Hidden Way of the East leads to the endless grassy plains rippling in the wind. The Hidden Way of the South leads to the White Hill crowned with radiant trees in the place of Light. The Hidden Way of the North leads to the dark ancient forests and the Sacred Mountain. The Hidden Way of the West leads to the murmuring realm of the ocean.

Stand at the center of the Four Hidden Ways, where all Directions come together as One, at the sacred marker stone. Sense, see, and feel, the Hidden Ways of East, South, North, and West. Let your mind pass along them in all directions, to the very ends of the human world, and the beginnings of the real world that lies beyond. Here is where all journeys begin, all journeys end. Here, at the Crossroads.

Know this: the Crossroads is also a meeting place, where many beings from different orders of life come together in equality and grace. It is our intention to meet with those Allies, Cousins, Co-Walkers and Spiritual Creatures, that are apt and willing to work with us in the task of redeeming the Surface World, to bring it closer and in harmony with the Primal World.

Be aware that they draw close, coming from the East, South, North and West. Some also rise up from the living land Beneath, at the center of the Crossroads. They draw close, to meet us where the Four Hidden Ways come together, at the center of all Directions.

(Music)

Be aware that you are at the Crossroads, in the presence of your Allies, Cousins, Co-Walkers and Companion Spiritual Creatures. You may return here always, in your dreams, visions, meditations, and waking consciousness. They draw close to you, embrace you, and commune with you. Join with them now in silence.

(Silent communion)

Be aware that, out of the Host that has gathered, certain beings come to you, apt and fitting to work with you. You do not choose them, they come to you.

Sense, see, and feel these beings, and form clearly in your mind that your intention is to work with them in the art and discipline of Faery Healing. Let all your thoughts rest upon this one task, and vow to undertake it to the utmost of your ability.

Now the Host begins to depart, and only your Close Companions remain. Declare to each of them that you with remember, realize, and return. They will each affirm their bond with you in their own manner.

Now open your eyes, so that you are at the Crossroads, but also aware of the outer world, wherever you may be. Rest upon the awareness that the Crossroads and your place in the outer world are one and the same, intertwined and inseparable.

Now be aware again of the Sky Above, the Land Below, and the Four Directions of the outer world. Be aware of what is in those Directions, be it city, oceans, open land; whatever is there, form it in your mind, see it, sense it, and feel it all about you.

As you return to the outer world, offer your thanks and respects to those Close Companions that have formed relationships with you. Acknowledge them to each of the Four Directions, and to the Land Below. Gradually their presence fades, and your presence in the human world increases.

Know that you may come and go freely, by way of the Crossroads, when you will. The Four Hidden Ways are open to you, and the Mysteries of the Directions will be revealed to you as you travel the Hidden Ways.

But for now, return to your human outer life. You have a Direction behind you, and Direction before you, and Directions to your right and left. And so you know your place, your way, and your potential.

With us is the Grace of the Shining Ones in the Mystery of Earth Light. Peace to all Signs and Shadows, Radiant Light to all Ways of Darkness, and the Living One of Light, Secret Unknown, Forever.

THE WELL OF ROSES

Our next form, also on the CD, is *The Well of Roses*. The Well of Roses is found in the initiatory ballad of *Tam Lin* (Appendix 1) and is discussed in many places in this book, especially in Chapter 7, *The Mystery of the Double Rose.* In this form or empowered vision, we work with the Well, the Roses, and the Three Heads. The motif of the Three Heads is found in both Faery tradition and in the Grail traditions. In all examples, the Heads embody and mediate spiritual forces of consciousness and transformation from the Faery realm and UnderWorld. The method is, as always, to use the motifs from traditional sources, and discover their inner power. In this manner, they become both sources of teaching and direct practical ways of experiencing the energies that they embody through image, association, and ancestral wisdom.

As with each of the empowered visions on the CD, work with this until it is clear in your memory, and you can do it anywhere, anytime, with or without the CD.

The Well of Roses

Be aware of the Sky Above, the Land Below, and the Four Directions of the Land. Be still, be ready.

Be aware now of the Great Forest that walks about the World: it is all about you, before you, behind you, to your right, to your left. The Great Forest that covered the Land before humans came; and that will cover the Land again when humans are gone. Wherever there is one splinter of wood, the Great Forest is with you – even amid the concrete, steel, and plastic of the city.

Feel the Great Forest surround you, and acknowledge its presence.

Build strongly before you the presence of the Well of Roses: see it, feel it, sense it. It is low well of dry-laid stones, surrounded by wild red and white briar rose bushes. The well is found in a natural open space in the heart of the Great Forest.

Our ancestors laid each stone of the wellhead long ago, surrounding a pure spring that rises from the radiant UnderWorld, the realm Below.

The first seeds of the red and white wild briar roses were brought here by the Faery allies to mark the compact and alliance between human and Faery races, to mark the redeeming powers of love and compassion.

It is said that if you have done one good deed in your life, even if you may not remember it, then the thorny bushes will part for you and you may approach the sacred well.

Draw near to the well: the thorny bushes part before you, and you come to the ancient stones. Here you give a gift. Whatever you find in your hands now, valuable or valueless, meaningful or meaningless, you give this unconditionally, placing it upon the stones of the well with no thought of benefit or return.

Out of the well rise three radiant heads: one of Copper, one of Silver, one of Gold. Commune with them, sense and feel their power and their presence.

(Silence, then music)

Be aware that you are at the sacred Well of Roses, in the heart of the Great Forest that walks about the World. You are in the presence of the Three Heads: Copper, Silver, and Gold. You may return here in your dreams, visions, and meditations.

Form clearly in you mind now that your intention is to develop your skill and aptitudes in Faery Healing. Approach each of the three in turn with this intention. First, the Copper Head (musical sound). Second, the Silver Head (musical sound). Third, the Gold Head (musical sound).

(Silence)

Now the power of the Three Radiant Heads flows through you. Let it fill your body and flow into your hands and feet. Sense the Four Hidden Ways within the shadows and light of the Forest, and merge them with the Four Directions of the surface world. Become aware of East, South, West, and North, the Sky Above, the Land Below. Be in two places at once: the sacred place of the Well of Roses, and the place in the outer world where you began your vision. Merge the two places as one within you.

Now the Three Heads fade, and you step back through the rose thicket. The forest fades, and you sense, see, and feel the out world.

Return to your outer awareness: open your eyes, breathe deeply, and remember all that occurred at the Well of Roses.

With us is the Grace of the Shining Ones in the Mystery of Earth Light. Peace to all Signs and Shadows, Radiant Light to all Ways of Darkness, and the Living One of Light, Secret Unknown, Forever.

THE HAWTHORN ROAD

The Hawthorn Road (also on the CD) is an ancient theme and narrative, albeit modernized in this presentation. In Appendix 2, you will find an initiatory song about the Hawthorn Road, from my recording *More Magical Songs*. With this empowered vision, we come into the Mystery of the Go-Betweens, those transhuman beings who live in the Faery realm and work with us in our tasks of Faery Healing and Earth Healing.

The Hawthorn Road

See, sense, and feel before you, the Hawthorn Road: two lines of dark trees, forming a tunnel, leaning over into one another, the thorny branches tangling, small leaves and white flowers.

Form this vision strongly before you, till all the outer human world fades into a mist and there is only you, standing in the mist, at the entrance to the Hawthorn Road. This is the Way.

Now you pass under the shadow of the hawthorn trees, and leave the world of time behind. The trail is rough and stony, and steep. Behind you is a gray mist, before you is the tunnel of trees, and at the far end, an arch of blue sky.

Climbing up the Hawthorn Road, you emerge on the side of a green hill. The air is clean, with clouds passing across the sky, and showers of rain. The light of the sun is clear, and you can see far across the land to a glimmer of ocean in the distance. There are tiny green fields surrounded by stone walls, narrow tracks, and no roads, no wires, no machines. This is Devon, in the west of England, in the 18th century.

The narrow path leads upwards to a cottage. Dug into the side of the hill, it has a turf roof and a single chimneystack. At the door an old woman stands to meet you. She has one blind eye and one seeing eye, and studies you closely with her blind eye. This is the Go-Between who will teach you the arts of Faery Healing. Form a clear intention in your mind that such is your wish, your dedication. Be still. Commune with her.

(Silence, then music)

Within the cottage there is but a single room: a large fireplace, a heavy wooden table, and many bags hanging from the roof beams. Two upright posts support the roof, made from the trunks of trees roughly shaped. On one a dark black knife is tied tightly with many loops of cord. Against the other leans a worn brown staff.

See, sense, and feel this room. Let it fill your memory, for you may return here in your dreams, visions, and meditations.

On the table is a large stone bowl of water, a pile of rounded pebbles, some bunches of dried and fresh herbs, three small sticks, and an aged black and red length of cord. Mark these well: touch them one by one, feel them and know them.

As you touch the objects on the table, the old woman leans across and places her hands upon yours: you touch them together. Form clearly your intention and dedication to bring the two worlds together, the first and primal world and the second and surface world, to effect healing and regeneration.

(Music, then silence)

Be aware that you are in the cottage on the hill with the wise woman, the Go-Between of our tradition. You may return here in your dreams, visions, and meditations. But now it is time for the outer world; and the old woman leads you out of the cottage and points down the hill. The hill is surrounded by a thick white mist, and it floats like a green island in the sea. The dark tunnel of hawthorn trees leads down into the mist, and you take that path.

Now you pass under the shadow of the hawthorn trees, and

descend down into the mist. You emerge into a shadow place, with shadow people. And you remember that you are one of those people, and so come back to your place in the outer world. The Hawthorn Road vanishes behind you, and you find yourself back where you began your visionary journey.

Hold to the memory of what happened, and return fully to your outer awareness. Know that you can travel the Hawthorn Road again.

You have a Direction behind you, and a Direction before you, and Directions to your right and to your left. The Sky Above, the Land Below. And so you have a sense of place, of potential.

With us is the Grace of the Shining Ones in the Mystery of Earth Light. Peace to all Signs and Shadows, Radiant Light to all Ways of Darkness, and the Living One of Light, Secret Unknown, reborn Forever.

THE OAK MYSTERY

The Mystery of the Sacred Kings and Priestess Queens

With this form we go deeper into the idea of, and communion with, those transhuman spiritual Go-Betweens that form a major part of all spiritual traditions. Whereas *The Hawthorn Road* is designed to put us into deep contact with one Go-Between, *The Oak Mystery* introduces us to a vast and enduring tradition. In Appendix 2, you will find *The Oak Song,* an initiatory song from my recording *More Magical Songs.*

The Oak Mystery (or The King in the Tree)

Communing with the Priest Kings and Priestess Queens

Be still, stilling time, space, and movement. Be aware of the Sky Above, and the living Land Below. Be aware of East, South, North, and West, the Directions before you, behind you, to your right and to your left. Be aware of the Flame of Being within that is at the Heart of All. Be still, at the center of the Seven Directions.

Now build strongly in your inner vision, and with all your senses, the presence of the ancient forest, the oak forest that was in the land before humans came, and will be in the land when humans are gone. The oak forest that walks around world by uttering seeds, which fall and grow into mighty trees that utter further seeds; thus does the forest walk about the world.

Know this: wherever there is one splinter of wood, the Great Forest is with you, even in the concrete heart of the city.

Sense, see, and feel the vast forest all about you. Feel the presence of the mighty oak trees, and of the many living creatures that dwell within the forest. Pass within, beneath the canopy of the trees, and tread lightly and respectfully here, for this is the home of the Faery races, the living creatures, and the ancestors. Long ago the mighty forest protected and nourished humanity, and the sacred oak tree has an especial care for humans, even now after the decimation and ruin.

Know that the trees have not gone, but can and will return when the fleeting works of man are changed, decayed, and forgotten. Know that the oak forest is ever present in the inner spirit world, and that you may bring it out into the outer wastelands. This is the Great Healing, between humans and the forest, and all that dwell therein.

Pass deeper within, and sense the herds of deer, the flocks of birds, and the invisible Faery guardians of the trees, tall noble warriors and wild savage maidens. Let them be your friends and allies if they will.

Be aware that each order of life has a king and queen here. In the animal realm, the king is the stag and the queen the doe. Sense, see, and feel the Mighty Stag: he leads you deeper into the forest, toward the Mystery at the Center, towards the oldest tree and its indweller and guardians.

Now the trees are wide and tall, each occupying a great space, until you come to a natural clear open circle. In the center of this is the oldest tree, a wide and venerable oak; so old, so mighty, that its roots have raised a hill, and out of the hill a clear stream of water flows. The spreading canopy of this oak stretches out to all Four Directions, and its crown reaches to the sky.

You sense many other beings here, visible or invisible; all are drawn to the tree and presence in the tree. Draw as close as you may.

As you approach the tree, the nine Priestess Queens appear before you, in a circle around the vast tree trunk. They are the Guardians of the Oak Mystery, and you may pass no further without their permission.

Be still, and reach into your true self. One or more of the Queens approaches you now, and sees deep, knowing all that you are and nothing may be hidden from them. One reaches out and makes a mark upon your brow. Now you may pass through the circle of the Guardians, the Priestess Queens, and approach the tree.

You climb the hill, over the raised mound of roots and rocks and earth, and you hear the running water of the clear spring. Draw close to the tree, and reach out to touch and embrace it. Feel its power flowing through your body, rising up through your feet to your head. Be still and merge with it.

Now you sense that there is someone in the tree, and looking up to where the huge branches open out, you see him. Reach up, as high as you may, stretching out your arm. He reaches down and grasps your hand, and hauls you up into the tree.

Be aware that you are in the presence of the King in the Tree. See, sense, and feel him, touch him, and he touches you. Things are very different here, where the Seven Directions come together, in this place that is above the Stars Below and below the Stars Above, neither on land nor sea, but partaking of all. Here time flows in and out of being, and the directions of East, South, North, and West, converge as one. Commune now with the Sacred King, and affirm that you have come in love and compassion to bring the primal land and the outer human lands close together in healing, redemption, and harmony. Be still, and commune a while in silence.

(Silent communion here)

Know that you are in the Mystery of the Oak Tree, in the presence of the Priest King and Priestess Queens. You may return here in your dreams, visions, and meditations, and this Mystery is always open to you.

The King looks upwards, and you follow his gaze. The oak tree grows up to the Moon, Sun and Planets, and Stars; and you rise up its towering branches, flowing up into the living cosmos. Be still and be at one.

From out beyond the Sun, at the threshold of the Stars, you sense again the world of your human birth, the planet Earth. With this sense you are drawn down, down through Sun and Moon, to the oceans and green lands of Earth. For a moment you feel and see it in its true eternal form, radiant with Earth Light, filled with Grace. Now you return to the place from whence you began your vision, and you come to the outer world again, the world of humans day-by-day, bound again by time. But you return with the knowledge that you may loose these bonds, and commune again with the Sacred King and the nine Priestess Queens.

Be aware of the Sky Above, the Land Below, and the Directions before you, behind you, to your right and to your left. Be still, knowing the being within. Hold to your memory of what happening in the oak tree, the mighty forest, in the primal world that heals and changes all.

With us is the Grace of the Shining Ones in the Mystery of Earth Light. Peace to all Signs and Shadows, Radiant Light to all Ways of Darkness, and the Living One of Light, Secret Unknown, reborn Forever.

THE SACRED MOUNTAIN

This is a longer form, and is in three stages. You should work, at first, with each stage individually and in order. When you have worked through all three, you can begin to combine them together. As always, I would encourage you to read through the entire visionary sequence before you try working deeply with it. This triple form will deepen your communion with the Living Creatures, the Ancestors, and the Shining Ones.

The Sacred Mountain

(1) The Hall of the Living Creatures.

Be still, and find yourself at the Crossroads.

Meet with your Allies, Cousins, and Co-Walkers, and merge in the Threefold Alliance of Human, Faery, and Living Creature.

Together you become the Streaming Host, a communion of power and presence that may travel where it wills.

Look to the North, along the Hidden Way of the North. There you will see a mighty snow capped mountain, with its towering crown truncated, for it is a dormant volcano. For the Streaming Host, to think is to move. You fly to the Sacred Mountain of the North, and find yourself standing before the entrance to a cavern.

Know this: there are Three Halls in the Mountain, first is the Hall of the Living Creatures, next the Hall of the Ancestors, and deep in the mountain roots, the Hall of the Shining Ones.

Form a clear intention in your mind that you will visit each of the Halls in turn. Begin with the Hall of the Living Creatures.

Pass through the cave along a winding way and come into a vast cavern lit by subtle light that rises from the earth and rock, beneath and all around. Here are many lush trees and flowering plants, coiling streams, and warm springs, wide deep lakes, waterfalls, and rocky hills within the mountain. This is the Hall of the Living Creatures. All creatures that have been in the world, are in the world, and will be the world yet to come, have their spiritual presence here.

Walk deeper in, and feel, sense, and see the many living beings that dwell in this timeless Hall of the Living Creatures. Birds, animals, fishes, insects, trees and plants: all are here.

Form a clear intention in your mind that you have come here to meet one of the Mentors, one of the Living Creatures that works to bring humanity and the other orders of life close together. As you form this intention, many creatures draw close all about you, touching you, resting on you. Be still and acknowledge their sacred presence.

To you now comes of the Mentors from the Living Creatures, and all others fall back before it. Commune with this being in silence.

Be aware that you are in the Hall of the Living Creatures, in the hidden cavern of the Sacred Mountain. Know that you may return here in your dreams visions and meditations

Note: after the communion you may return out of the cavern, back to the Crossroads, and so to the outer world. If you do this, you return again via the Crossroads and the Streaming Host, and pass through the Hall of the Creatures towards the Hall of the Ancestors. This is described next. If you do not return, you proceed on to the second hall to meet the Ancestors:

(2) The Hall of the Ancestors

Your Mentor Creature leads you by winding pathways, deep into the timeless realm of the Living Creatures. You come at last to a low tunnel in the rock, and this you must enter. As you do so, form a clear intention in your mind that you are going towards the Hall of the Ancestors.

You climb down this sloping narrow way on hands and knees, and emerge into a shadowy cavern with a wide dark river running through it. By the banks of the river there is small campfire burning in a ring of stones, with the First Ancestors sitting around it. They are no more in number than grandparents, parents, and children.

The children see and sense you, and lead you to the fire. To them you are spirits from the end of time; to you they are the First Ancestors at the dawn of time. Sit awhile and commune with them in silence.

Be aware that you are in the Hall of the Ancestors, deep in the center of the Sacred Mountain. Know that you may return here in your dreams, visions, and meditations.

Note: at this point you may return through the narrow way, through the Hall of the Creatures to the Crossroads and so back to the outer world. When you return, you retrace your steps and proceed as follows:

(3) The Hall of the Shining Ones

The ancestral children bid you go to the dark river, and you see a faint path along its shore, worn into the rock of the cavern. You follow this down a long high tunnel, and the dark river grows wide and strong. In the distance you hear a roaring sound: know that this is one of the two rivers of the UnderWorld, and that it falls in a mighty waterfall into the heart of the Earth.

Now you emerge on the very edge of that waterfall, where it flows out of the face of the precipice, and down into the Earth Light. The light radiates upwards, all about you. Looking down you see the Shining Ones in the heart of the Earth.

They appear as a lattice of shifting pattern and colors, weaving many complex shapes of light. You sense that there are Seven Great Ones, and many lesser ones that partake of them. Be still, stilling time, space, and movement, and come into communion with the Shining Ones, who weave the dream of the world in the Earth Light.

(Pause here for silent communion)

Be aware that you are in the Hall of the Shining Ones, deep in the Earth Light at the roots of the Sacred Mountain. Know that you may return here in your dreams, visions, and meditations.

With us is the Grace of the Shining Ones in the Mystery of Earth Light. Peace to all Signs and Shadows, Radiant Light to all Ways of Darkness, and the Living One of Light, Secret Unknown, reborn Forever.

BRIDGE MAKING

Go to the Crossroads, and come into your Threefold Alliance.

See, sense, and feel the Well of Light open out at the center, where the Four Hidden Ways come together.

A Go-Between emerges from the Well of Light and bids you descend into the UnderWorld. You pass far down into the living body of the land, and the power of your Threefold Alliance makes that journey light, to all three. You see, sense, and feel the Go-Between, leading the way.

Whatever you perceive on your journey, know that you come at last to a place where there is a wide rift, where the deep body of the land or ocean floor has been torn apart. This is a rift of the life forces of the Earth, and not merely a rift of the rock.

Commune awhile with and through the Go-Between. Form a clear intention that you have come here to build a bridge across the rift, and set the healthy flow of Earth power in circulation here.

As you form this intention, you sense, see, and feel many beings arrive to be with you. In this world intention is *all*, and they have sensed your intention, and so they respond. They gather around you in a swirling pattern, ready to work with you.

Out of the depths of the ravine, a large spirit being rises. You may not see it clearly, but you sense its presence. It stretches its body across the gap, and many other creatures stream into it and merge with it. You must give something of yourself to this bridge, for each order of life must be present for it to hold.

Give unconditionally of yourself to make the bridge, and be still. Commune awhile in silence. Sense what flows across the Bridge.

Be aware that you are deep in the UnderWorld, in the act of Bridge Making. Form a clear intention that you will be ready to contributed to further Bridge Making, as part of your work in Earth Healing.

Now you return to the surface world, rising up within your Three-fold Alliance. For a moment you see, sense, and feel the new bridge below you, then it is closed to you. You return to the Crossroads and, from there, back to the outer world.

With us is the Grace of the Shining Ones in the Mystery of Earth Light. Peace to all Signs and Shadows, Radiant Light to all Ways of Darkness, and the Living One of Light, Secret Unknown, reborn Forever.

PART TWO

7. The Mystery
of the Double Rose

The rose is the major flower in Faery tradition, found in British and European sources ranging from humble folktales, to the imagery and pagan foundations of the original Rosicrucian tracts of the 16th Century (which should not be confused with the later fraternal and neo-Masonic Rosicrucian groups, or the present day AMORC, founded in the 20th Century). The rose is also central to traditions of the *jinn* and the otherworld that come from Persia or the Middle East, from whence its mystical and magical connections reached to India with the Moghul empire. In our present context we are mainly concerned with the rose in the northern and western Faery traditions, those of Europe, Britain, and Ireland, and the important connections to those traditions within American folklore. Such connections originally arose and remained due to the influence of the Scottish-Irish emigrants and slaves, who brought the Faery tradition, folk tales, narrative ballads, and folkloric magical and healing practices with them from their home countries. Although contemporary people recreate Faery and pagan magic, the living folkloric traditions should, and must, be the foundation for everything that is recreated. Such traditions are the wisdom of the ancestors, and comprise an enormous resource for us, providing we know how to work with them.

THE DELUSION OF SYMBOLISM

Before we work with the Mystery of the Double Rose, we must clear our minds of some assumptions that permeate modern thinking. The spiritual and physical rose is not merely a symbol or allegory, even though we may sometimes find levels of both when we explore what is taught about the rose. The rose in Faery tradition, as in Sufi or Rosicrucian mysticism, is an entity, a spiritual being, and a spiritual power. Indeed, many aspects of the original Rosicrucian imagery of the 16th Century spring from Germanic folklore and classical mythology regarding the goddess Venus and the rose; while Sufi poetry and mystical teachings involving roses are often based upon the ancient tradition of spiritual love and of loving relationship with the Faery beings, the *jinn*. In all cases, the rose is not a symbol or a hidden message, but the embodiment of a divine power, a power that flows through both the flower itself and through the Threefold Alliance of humanity, the Faery races, and the living creatures. In the *Golden Ass* by Roman author Apuleius, an initiatory text often described as the first magical novel, the hero may be cured of his transformation into an ass only by eating roses – not by interpreting the symbolism of the rose, but by eating physical roses. The rose is an entity, a being with intense spiritual power. An online edition of *The Golden Ass*, based on a classic 16th Century translation, may be found at http://eserver.org/books/ apuleius/default.html.

Modern magic has lost much of the immediacy and physicality of traditional magic. This is due to the influence of both popular psychology and fantasy entertainment, whereby powerful entities have become thought of as "symbols" or "archetypes," or are "all in the mind."

This concept of the rose as a power source and entity is best understood today within the idea of flower essences, a therapy that comes directly from Faery tradition, in which essences of dew from plants have been used for centuries (see the section on *Flower Essences and Faery Tradition* in Chapter 3). The living plant embodies and mediates complex subtle forces, and these have a transformative effect upon us. They change us because we have *something within us* that resonates in tune with those forces embodied and mediated in the plant world by the rose. They do not change us through attempts to interpret symbolism or a psychological assessment of romantic impulses.

To discover what that *something within* may be, we can explore the clues, teachings, and descriptions handed down to us from the Faery and UnderWorld traditions. Before doing so, we must first define and assess the meaning of "tradition," for this world has gradually had its meaning changed in general usage, and the changes are not to our benefit.

THE TRUTH ABOUT TRADITIONS

Please remember that when we refer to "traditions" in this context, we mean ancestral traditions, and not modern teachings associated with revival paganism or witchcraft. It is widespread nowadays for modern pagans or witches to say "in our tradition," when they really mean "in our specific line of practices and teachings." These lines can, and often do, derive from ancestral traditions (sometimes several at once), but they are modern extensions and are not the ancestral traditions in themselves.

So before going further into evidence and its spiritual and magical implications for the Double Rose and for Faery Healing, we should establish a basic definition of tradition and its sources. This is vitally important for us, if we are to understand what is at the foundation of Faery tradition, and of Faery Healing. The traditions that we rest upon, and eventually build upon, are those described in various ways in ancient source texts from classical, European, and certain broadly Celtic origins. The material found scattered through such source texts is then compared with folkloric practices, Faery tales, and folk ballads and songs that speak of the Faery themes: such material was originally written down or collected from oral folkloric tradition.

A folkloric tradition is always unconscious, and is never part of a pagan revival. Indeed, anyone who declares something like "what I practice is part of an ancient unbroken tradition" is either deluded or lying. But someone who says, "my line of practices and teachings relates strongly to ancestral traditions" has integrity and probably speaks the truth. Anyone within a true folkloric magical tradition will say nothing about it at all, for such traditions are *unconscious* and are integrated deeply into daily life in such a way that only an outsider might recognize them as magical arts.

The folkloric sources are the traditions that provided both the content and impetus for the current revival of pagan spirituality in its many variants. They are the foundation. When we find coherent connections between the old source texts and the folkloric material, and where we find related concepts described in both, and employed by ordinary people (not pagan revivalists) in folkloric magic, these connections and concepts are the indicators of enduring Faery and UnderWorld traditions. There is a wealth of such evidence. We are fortunate indeed to have texts from the medieval period onwards, and folkloric collections ancient and modern, which preserve material on the traditions. From this point, the modern revival can, and does, take over. Ideally, modern magic, witchcraft, and paganism in its many variants should rest upon a well-studied foundation of ancestral tradition – and not rely merely upon the specially written studies, papers, and books generated within the custom and practices of any one group, temple, coven, or network.

This connection to ancestral tradition is important, not merely from the perspective of accuracy, history, and knowledge, but for another reason. If we attune to the consciousness of the ancestors, their wisdom and power flows to us. If we attune to their traditional arts of magic, we reconnect with those traditions and share their knowledge. This task involves, at the beginning, careful and accurate study. It is our acquired accurate knowledge of the traditions that builds the framework within with our magical work is supported and developed, and which is gradually empowered by the living consciousness of the *inner tradition*. If that knowledge is inaccurate or whimsical, the framework will be weak, and the inner tradition will not be supported by it. In other words, we are losing the old traditions day by day, and any revivals must be accurate and faithful to what we know. Otherwise we are just playing games, inflating egos, creating false spirituality.

So let us move on to a short summary of the roots of the Double Rose in Faery and UnderWorld tradition.

THE DOUBLE ROSE

In the Scottish Faery ballad of *Tam Lin*, the rose appears in conjunction with some very specific Faery elements: the sacred hill, the wood, the well, and the lovers. Young Janet pulls "a double rose" to summon Tam Lin from the spirit world, in order that he might make love to her. As always, we should consider this ballad not as mere symbolism, but as having a deep practical meaning and methods for magical transformation of energy and consciousness. This is how the old Faery tradition was taught and experienced: through tales and songs which, if the individual understood the esoteric content, could be "activated" into dynamic processes of change, into ritual, and into communion with the Faery races and the living spiritual creatures.

While to the romantic poet, the rose eventually came to symbolize true love in a stylish convention, this idea of stock symbolism is a weak remnant of the original spiritual power inherent in the rose. (C.S. Lewis points out some of the traps and fallacies of attaching psychological or other modern ideas of symbolism to older texts and concepts in his book *The Allegory of Love* (Oxford University Press; Reprint edition, November 1985). While Lewis' aim is to study the development of romantic poetry, and would thoroughly disapprove of this present text on Faery Healing, his learned and perceptive comments on this retro-trap are invaluable to the modern magician.

By thinking of anything as a "symbol" we distance ourselves from it, make it into a product observed by the rational mind that looks for a category of meaning, rather than live within the deeper imagination and spiritual awareness that looks for presence and power.

Yet, we may explore the traditions associated with the rose through the association, in traditional ballads, with love and death. This is commonly assumed to be formulaic romanticism, but it is not. In a number of folkloric ballads and tales, the theme of True Lovers is found. This is, of course, also the theme of *Tam Lin*, one of the great initiatory mysteries of the Faery tradition. Other ballads focus more in the love and death motifs, without the Faery content. In these, the basic plot appears to be simple: there are two lovers, and for various reasons depending on the ballad, first one dies, then the other. Though they are separated by the vagaries of life and love, they are united in death. They are buried near to one another, and from the grave of one a red rose grows, and from the other, a white rose. These are, traditionally, wild briar roses, which have a trailing growth, rather than the cultivated rose bush of the modern garden. The red and white rose plants intertwine in a true lovers' knot, and the lovers are united beyond the grave. Indeed, they are embodied within and become the red and white rose bushes. Traditionally the white rose is of the male, and the red of the female.

This might seem to be nothing more than romantic style, and indeed it can be taken at that level of understanding, which was superficially satisfying to the listener. But if we pursue the idea of the double rose through the more specific initiatory ballads of *Tam Lin* and *Thomas Rhymer*, we find a deeper mystery revealed. This mystery is relevant to the entire tradition, but also, in our present context, to the experience, power, and practice of Faery Healing.

ROSES, RIVERS, AND DRAGONS

At a deeper level the red and white rose relate to those two rivers in the UnderWorld, described in the ballad of *Thomas Rhymer*, as a river of blood and a river of tears. These streams appear also in folkloric songs that relate to the Grail tradition, such as *Down in Yon Forest* (in which streams of water and blood flow from the side of a wounded sleeping knight), and they have an implied presence, occasionally stated in the Grail texts themselves. In the early

Christian sources, they are thought of in the context of the wounds of Christ, revealing the pagan origins of the Christian mystery. But the concept of the streams of blood and water is ancient, and ultimately is found in UnderWorld traditions.

The river of blood sustains the white rose, while the river of tears sustains the red rose. They cannot exist without one another.

In terms of humanity, the white rose refers the polarity of subtle forces within the male body, and the red to the subtle forces of the female body. These polarities derive, at a very deep level, from the red and white dragons, which are so vividly described in the 12th Century *Prophecies of Merlin*, as ceaselessly interacting in the UnderWorld.

The red and white dragons, the primal powers interacting, then the rivers of blood and tears, which are those same powers in circulation, and the red and white roses which are associated with human love and sex, are all manifesting and mobile aspects of planetary forces, below and within earth and sea, which in turn, reflect cosmic forces. In the ultimate sense, these are the forces of creation and destruction, or of Severity and Mercy, the Powers of Giving and of Taking.

Thus, the unrequited lovers of seemingly romantic ballads and tales embody, at the deepest level, the working out of planetary and cosmic forces. As do we all.

The Mystery of the Double Rose is a polarity mystery. We may begin with the traditional clues, images, and practical teachings of the Faery and UnderWorld traditions, as described above. We may progress towards a greater concept and reality, that of cosmic forces of creation and destruction. But in practice we should be concerned with the effects, results, and potentials of this traditional wisdom teaching.

When you are working in the Faery tradition, never forget that it is not a philosophy or a religion; it is a practical tradition about relationships between humanity, other orders of life, and the planet. Regrettably, one of the early academic source texts of the 20th Century, the first book by American scholar W.Y. Evans-Wentz, was titled *The Fairy Faith in Celtic Countries*. The title of this otherwise admirable and helpful thesis has led to the common assertion today that there is a "Fairy Faith," or was such a faith in the past – as if the Faery tradition was a religion. There is, however, no faith and no worship in Faery tradition. There is relationship, interaction, and certain well-defined customs and practices. There is no "belief" in Faeries, as their presence is known and proven by experience; and there never were, nor are there today, priests or priestesses of any Faery or fairy faith, other than contemporary claimants who reveal their ignorance of the tradition by making such claims. Anyone can be a priest or priestess, according to the best of their ability, but not of a non-existent Faery religion.

The Faery tradition, which is really an amalgam of several strands of ancient magical traditions, has as its practitioners, seers and seeresses, and healers as its specialists, along with storytellers and singers, and overall participants. There is no hierarchy, no authority, and no edifices, temples, rulebooks, or liturgies. What a relief!

The Mystery of the Double Rose is about polarity. Before going deeper into the mystery, we must be clear that we are not dealing with stereotypes of male and female (as in romanticism), but working directly with forces that occur within each and every one of us, regardless of physical gender or sexual orientation. There will be a tendency for the male body to express the powers of the white rose, and for the female to express the powers of the red, but each has both within. Thus, the simple polarities of the Faery tales and ballads are not to be understood as rules or dogma, but as *indicators of how things work*. Once we have activated the esoteric content and methods, these polarities can (and do) change.

We may work with the indicators found within ancestral tradition on several levels. In the list and exploration that follows, remember that the roses are both polarities and entities, and energies embodied by plants. The flowers are both the sexual organs of the plants, and the organs of spiritual communication: this double function should provide much insight in meditation.

The levels of consciousness and energy are broadly as follows, bearing in mind that there are no hard boundaries between them, and that they interlace with one another in many ways:

1. We may work with the red and white rose powers within ourselves (red and white roses, blood, and water/semen). Such work would be with the body, with health and well being, with physical skills, and with inner meditations on our subtle forces.

2. In relationship to other humans, as in (1) – Here we open out to contact with others; this will include creative, communicative, and sexual unions and relationships. At the deepest levels, this will include magical and spiritual polarity relationships with other humans.

3. In relationship to other beings, as in the Threefold Alliance (the subtle energies of the roses and the fluids) – Here we open out to, commune with, and make relationships with the other orders of life. The Threefold Alliance involves a relationship between humans (which may include spiritual ancestors and genetic ancestors), the Faery allies, and the living creatures such as birds, animals, fishes, and insects). In many cases, the Faery and creature companions are spirit beings, metaphysical entities. But sometimes the alliance will bridge over into a special relationship with certain creatures and plants that are found in the manifest world of nature, as these are the outer forms for the inner contacts.

4. A deep relationship with, and ongoing work within, the subtle life and death forces of the land or sea (the Rivers of Blood and Tears) – This relationship is, at first, initiatory. It brings transformation. It is typified in the initiatory ballad of *Thomas Rhymer*, in which the Faery Queen shows the poet the Rivers, during a journey to the UnderWorld. After his journey and seven years in service to the Queen, the poet becomes a prophet.

This fourth level gradually becomes a resource for specific tasks of Earth Healing, whereby the forces of the mighty rivers are available to us, usually working with allies, to strengthen and empower actions such as bridge making, death transitions, and prophetic vision.

5. With the deep planetary forces (the Red and White Dragons) – At this level the human consciousness no longer functions in terms of day-to-day personality. Instead, we come into the

rhythms of long-term cycles of energy and long phases of planetary life. At this depth we work with wordless understanding of the movement of the world, of weather, of communion with the stars.

6. With the cosmic forces embodied in the planetary forces – This level is usually discerned at first as a vision or sense of stars within the UnderWorld. In myth, some of these forces are found in the Titans; not the surfacing energies of the Titans that cause movement such as tidal waves, volcanoes, and earthquakes (which are mainly at the 5th level described above), but the deeper sources of their power. In mythic history, Titans were originally paired deities, male/female, mediating cosmic forces through the planets of the solar system. At a certain phase in the solar life, they passed out of the planets into the UnderWorld of Earth. This is rationalized and preserved in the story of the Titans being "cast out" by the Olympians, who become the planetary deities. This story reminds us, with more detail, of the legends of Lucifer in Christian tradition, or of Iblis in the Islamic tradition.

7. Communion with the source of Earth Light at One – At this deepest stage, the seventh level, we lose the polarity of the Red and White. Here we commune with the source of the Earth Light, that stellar consciousness that is deep within the planet.

WHAT IS HEALING?

There are many ways to understand, and undertake, healing. In this book, we are primarily concerned with spiritual forces and Faery Healing, an art in which humans and metaphysical beings work together. But to truly come into this art, to form a positive working relationship with our allies, we must give some thought to what healing is. This chapter explores a definition of healing from spiritual perspective, often in contrast to a materialistic perspective. As humans, we experience both. Our emphasis here is the positive effects of Faery Healing, by which we mean not merely end results, but the effects of consciousness.

So what is healing? The most obvious, direct, and yet most subtle answer is that *healing is a process whereby imbalances are restored to balance.*

However, if we take a human-centric view, and then an ego-centric view, our idea of balance immediately becomes exclusive. Balance becomes "my balance," and is related to individual benefit. This leads inevitably to the modernist situation whereby the short-term benefit, the quick fix, is all, even at the expense of the surrounding environment. As long as we feel good, nothing else matters.

To go further into this situation, we might consider a practical example. If an area of land is over populated, over farmed, over exploited, it will boom for some years. Everyone has enough to eat and feels good. But eventually, the land becomes depleted, imbalanced, and ceases to produce. This imbalance affects every living creature in the land, not merely the humans, and creates a feedback pattern whereby the destructive spiral accelerates. The human population suffers from malnourishment, disease, and eventually begins to decline. They may even die out altogether. Yet, it was the human presence and practices that created the imbalance – so the decline of the human population is the rebalancing, the death is the healing.

The same model applies to the individual, to me and to you: death is the process that heals the long-term imbalances and toxins of the life.

So when we think of healing as a process of coming into balance and coming out of imbalance, we have to consider where we set the thresholds. In our theoretical example above, one man with a supply of stored food, drugs, supplements, and anti-biotics could live out the famine and disease. But, would he be balanced?

The individual life story mirrors the greater life story of a place, a collective, or a planet. What level, what community of balances and imbalances, do we address in the process of healing? And, as individuals, how much should we accept or reject of the communities or networks of imbalance that surround us?

There Are Three Kinds of Healing

Materialistic medicine is dedicated to the healing of the individual human. Nothing else matters, and all is considered fair in the war against disease, pain, illness, and death. This very focused approach, developed over the last two hundred years of scientific research, has produced remarkable techniques, especially in the field of surgery. This is combative healing and requires a specific materialistic perspective and dedication. Its origin is, of course, in compassion for the individual, no matter how we might question the commercialized interests that control medicine in society. One of the key concepts in this type of healing is speed: it has to be done as quickly as possible to obtain immediate or rapid beneficial results that can be seen, felt, defined, and appreciated.

Holistic medicine is also dedicated to the healing of the individual human. In holistic approaches to healing, of which there are many, the idea of combat is reduced, and the tendency is to work towards balancing the entire individual, rather than fighting overt and manifest symptoms. At its deeper levels, holistic medicine works with complex and subtle relationship between the individual and his/her environment, something that is usually ignored as irrelevant in materialistic medical practices. In this type of healing, a longer term approach is often found, and the quick fix is not sought so much as the deep fix, even if it takes longer to achieve.

Spiritual healing, whatever the tradition, begins out of time. This is the most important concept, whatever tradition of spiritual healing we may choose to work with. The Faery tradition is no different in this respect: the healing obviates the usual cycles of time. Our immediate sense of this is through the dramatic instant healings reported from tradition, whereby wounds close up, or intrusions are removed from the body. Time is irrelevant in such healings. But this is only a mere fraction of the potential, for spiritual healing works with a much larger perspective of time, energy, and interaction.

In Faery Healing we work with the Threefold Alliance of human, Faery, and living creature. This in itself is deeply healing, for it brings *all three* orders of life into harmony with one another. With this one root concept and interaction, we suddenly find an entire world of insights into healing opening out for us. It is no longer about the human individual "feeling better," but about communion and consciousness, about *being in the world in an entirely different way*. This idea of a *healing change of context* applies to all three orders of life in the Threefold Alliance, not just to the humans – mutual exchange, mutual benefit.

FROM TRADITION TO EARTH HEALING

Before we can explore this theme in depth, and discover its practical implications, both in the art of Faery Healing, and in our own lives, we must first explore what "tradition and Earth Healing" mean, here. Both are phrases used very widely, sometimes indiscriminately, in the current revival of interest in spirituality and magic. And, as we know only too well, words like tradition and healing are often ruthlessly abused in manipulative advertising and political and religious propaganda.

WHAT IS TRADITION?

Our definitions are going to be strict and conservative, at least in terms of the actual words *tradition* and *Earth Healing*. Surprisingly, or not, a simple conservative definition is often a surprise to many people, as they accept the loose and ambiguous definitions that are widely used in media, popular books, and general conversation about such subjects. We live in an age when many fine definitions and potent concepts through words have been hijacked and even twisted to mean their opposites. Just listen to any political speech, or view commercial advertising in the media. But, this runs much deeper than the lies of politicians or the banal drivel of advertising.

When most people live in world of sound bites and pop definitions, they lose vocabulary. When we lose vocabulary, we lose the vehicle for thought. When we lose the vehicle for thought, we lose the means for expressing ourselves. When we cannot express ourselves – bingo! We are exactly where we can do least harm to vested interests, those same vested interests that created the artificial world in the first place. It is not a conspiracy so much as a neo-organic network of obfuscation posing as a cornucopia of modernist benefits. "Be the person you really are." "Express yourself through your furniture." "Modern living for the way you are today." "The tradition of …"

Such vague pseudo-meaningful phrases are the children of other word abuse, some of which has greatly transformed the way modern people think. The word "archetype," everyone knows, refers to certain key images in the psyche: the Father, the Goddess, the Strong Man, the Flower Maiden, and so forth. But, this meaning is very contemporary and was coined by C.G. Jung, who took a Greek word and gave it a meaning of his own. An archetype, up until less than 100 years ago, meant a cosmic matrix, mold, or shaping force, out of which inherent patterns of creation were shaped, that led to groups of manifestation that had many relationships, due to their archetypal origins in the spiritual or cosmic realm.

Thus a powerful tool for conceptualizing has been minimized in use in therapy to refer solely to aspects of the human psyche. The Jungian and post-Jungian archetype is something very different from the true meaning of the word. The word has been hijacked, its meaning changed in a manner that denies us its original meaning.

I have spent some space on this example, because the same thing has occurred with the word "tradition," albeit in a very different way and for quite different reasons. But the shifting ground of meaning, which shifts away from depth towards the shallows, is still present.

A *tradition* is something that has been going on for a long time, handed down from the ancestral past. It is not a custom or a pattern that has been created by any one person or group within one lifetime. The key definition of tradition is that *it has no author or originator*: this is what makes it traditional. Legislation is founded upon, and recognizes, the significance of this definition in copyright, for if there is an author there is a copyright. But if a source is traditional, there is no copyright. It has no owner, no originator.

This idea of tradition as something anonymous and collective is vitally important for those of us who work with the spiritual impetus of ancestral wisdom. In revival paganism and witchcraft, many groups and individuals use the phrase "in our tradition," when in fact they are referring to the exclusive *custom and practice* of their group or network, which is often *defined by texts by specific authors*. Anyone referring to a tradition in this manner of conscious self-identification is not in a tradition, for tradition does not identify itself as such – it merely is. Nor can we criticize such assertions blindly, for they are made out of innocence, through ignorance of the true nature of tradition. More simply, the term "tradition" has been hijacked in the last 50 years or so, and is on its way towards losing its deeper and much more valuable meaning.

The majority of revival spirituality and magic is, strictly speaking, *custom and practice defined by texts by specific authors*. Such texts can be private manuscripts or ritual books, or can be published items that are widely read. When I refer to the Faery tradition, I am referring to a collective of ancestral traditions and folkloric practices, mainly from Europe, Britain, and Ireland, but with many parallels and interconnections worldwide. I am not referring to the "R.J. Stewart Faery Tradition" There is no such thing, no matter how much original text I publish as an author, and no matter how many rituals or visualizations I create to help us all come into a deeper relationship with the Faery tradition.

Modern specific magical or spiritual group identities often associate themselves with ancestral traditions: Roman, Greek, Strega, Norse, Celtic, and so forth. Thus the Faery tradition that we are dealing with in this book is, broadly speaking, Celtic. But there are many connections to Italian, Norse-Germanic, Greek, Persian, and many other traditions, as Faery magic is at the foundation of all magic.

However, the greater ancestral traditions are *cultural and historical*, covering very wide territories indeed, and they cannot be truly specified within a relationship to modern pagan custom and practice. They can, and most certainly do, help to define a certain broad cultural affinity within a modern pagan or magical group, but cannot be claimed as traditions in themselves, especially not as traditions to which a group or individual "belongs." The ancestral traditions are cultural and historical collectives, reported mainly in literature and archaeology, which embrace many varied sub-traditions of life, magic, folklore, and ethnic practices.

Sometimes the intelligent reports, which form the basis for our modern ideas about ancestral traditions, are anthropological or from folklore studies, and some certainly contain content from the remnants of living magical folkloric traditions. We might think of classic examples such as the collection of Gaelic prayers, *Carmina Gaedelica*, or Leland's *Aradia* reporting the practices of Italian folkloric magic. Then there are other, more modern, examples that are much less certain of origin and always hotly debated. In these we have charismatic individuals who intentionally create modern revivals of paganism, sometimes based on research into ancient practices and, what comes next is most important in our discussion, they also *claim to have received some material direct from living folkloric traditional sources*. The most famous example is probably Gerald Gardner, though many more can be cited. We can use Gardner as an example of the one who stands for many in this process, without any disrespect either to him or to the many.

Gardner studied many aspects of magic folklore and anthro-pology, and created a new set of *customs and practices* deriving from *cultural and historical* evidence in literature and included, as he asserts, material remnants of a living anonymous tradition of folk magic in England. Thus he produced a set of rituals, which today have many relatives and variants, and which have become widespread *custom and practice defined by text by a specific author*: this material has been a major influence on the revival of witchcraft, paganism, and magic. It is almost always referred to as the "Gardnerian tradition," which is a self-canceling definition, as an author cannot be the source of a tradition, only the ancestral collective can be such a source. Once again, this analysis is not disrespectful to Gardner: one of my first introductions to someone mediating the Goddess was in ritual with Patricia Crowther, a priestess of great power, who was trained and initiated by Gerald Gardner.

At this stage in the exploration of tradition, I must state firmly that I do not discuss any of the above comments on contemporary claims about "in our tradition" out of cynicism. Indeed, I have no doubt that many aspects of the pagan and magical revival derive from and, more importantly, tap into the spirit of the ancestral consciousness. Without pivotal figures like Gardner and many others, the revival would not have gained such impetus and energy. But, if we are to go forward and define an ongoing and deepening future potential for our spirituality, we must stop thinking and saying that specific *practices and texts* are "traditions." By doing so, we deprive ourselves of a source of spiritual power, wisdom, and insight. We lose our sense of the ancestral consciousness embodied in the true and anonymous collective traditions of each land.

We deprive ourselves by assuming that a tradition is only a defined set of methods with a label. And, no matter how fine and powerful such a set may be, it is at best, a subset of modern *customs and practices* created out of a cultural and historical ambience drawing upon defined sources (Norse, Celtic, Greek, Italian, Finnish, and so forth).

This raises the entire question of education within pagan and wiccan or magical groups, many of which are legally recognized religious organizations. For the ongoing and growing trend towards self-reference as an authority (In Our Tradition) leads us away from the mighty ocean of ancestral wisdom towards small islands of an increasingly politicized, limited, and exclusive custom and practice. In other words, a pagan group, church, temple, or organization begins to increasingly resemble those very self-referring structures that they sought to replace – those politicized religions that refer only to themselves as sole sources of authority.

In a broader sense, of course, this is fate of any highly organized human group, be it a corporation, a political party, or a church or temple. But we are talking about *spiritual traditions* here, not fiscal practices or (horror of horrors!) dogma.

Having explored some definitions of healing and of tradition, let us move on to the deeper concept of Earth Healing.

WHAT IS EARTH HEALING?

In several chapters of this book, we explore the relationship between traditions and practices of Faery Healing, and healing in general. In this section, we will go deeper into this relationship, especially by exploring and defining, as much as possible, the concept of Earth Healing.

In our current time of environmental crisis, or rather crises (plural), it has become fashionable to talk grandly about "planetary healing." Earth Healing is just that, healing of the planet. It is the deepest level of healing that there may be, and we would be poseurs if we claimed to be able to achieve it alone. The New Age movement is full of grandiose claims of healing and ascension, which seem to inflate the ego, rather than come close to a true ethical and spiritual transformation. Anyone seriously working on planetary healing must first admit, to himself or herself, that is a long-term task with no immediate personal benefit.

When we come to this inevitable conclusion, we are not alone. Our ancestors, who built the stone circles and alignments, did not build them for themselves. Consider that these sacred sites often took centuries, generations, to build. The ancestors built them not for themselves, but for us, the generations of the future. So when we work on spiritual tasks we are working for future generations, just as our ancestors did. This concept, this method, this truth, puts us into a deep stream of spiritual awareness that transcends time and opens us to the wisdom resources of the ancestors. More simply we might say this: the short-term fix, the short-term aim for gain, profit, and self, has failed, so let's focus on discovering and then implementing the long-term truth. Where do we begin? Probably with the admission that we do not know what this long-term truth of planetary healing may become, then with the commitment that we are willing to work towards it, unconditionally.

Earth Healing is not merely about cleaning up pollution, re-plenishing the ozone layer, planting more trees, or allowing creatures to live naturally once more. All of these aims are essential, worthwhile, and good, but they deal with symptoms rather than causes. Until we have a change of awareness on a very large scale, we are merely cleaning up a mess, a task that seems ever greater and more daunting to the workers. So Earth Healing, while cleaning up the mess, must also be about a change of awareness.

We think of such changes, appropriately, as necessary for human awareness, both individual and collective. Such a revolution of humanity towards an ethical self-preservation seems to be essential now for our survival as a species. Once upon a time it might have been a matter of higher ethics, but now it is urgent and upon us – do it or die.

In the Faery tradition, there is a long established pattern of co-operation between humans, Faery beings, and living creatures...*conscious co-operation*. If we are to seriously embark upon our share of Earth Healing, the deepest level of Faery Healing, it must be a co-operative venture. To enter into this co-operation, we must establish relationships with the larger organs of the planetary Being. These are defined in ancestral tradition as Giants or Titans. The first definition is Norse-Teutonic; the second is Greek and even pre-Greek in origin. Both describe vast and powerful beings that are at the foundations of the creation of the planet, and are associated with planetary forces such as massive storms, earthquakes, volcanoes, polar ice, and so forth. Similar concepts and beings are found in all the folkloric traditions world-wide, and play a significant role in ancestral and esoteric mystical and religious lore, methods, and initiations.

Of course, the materialist or modern rationalist assumes all of the above to be simplistic imagery to account for natural phenomenon, to which superstition or fears have been attached, accumulating through the generations. Yet, ancestral tradition does not merely use myths of these vast beings to explain why an earthquake occurs, though that idea is indeed present at a superficial level. In the accounts of both Giants and Titans, there is a clear connection between the planetary forces and the cosmic forces of creation and destruction. So rather than being a simplistic rationalization of fears, the descriptions of Giants and Titans provide deep mythic insights into levels of planetary interaction within itself, and how such interactions resonate with the greater entities of the cosmos.

It has been a common assumption for the last 200 years (by the sciences of "Western" culture) that myths are the product of ignorance. A similar assumption was made by the founders of the psychological movement in the late 19th Century, who assumed that myths and Faery tales were traditional embodiments of the collective and individual psyche or that, at best (as assumed by Jung), that they were a kind of proto-psychology that could be subsumed under the new therapeutic insights and methods.

Myths, Faery tales, and legends all embody a way of describing the relationship between humans, the planet, and other orders of life. Much of this wisdom is also found, albeit in differing presentations, in perennial esoteric traditions of the world, though this is often ignored or repudiated by scientists and scholars alike. Both the Greek philosophers and the medieval Qabalists adequately described the interactions of time, space, and energy centuries before New Physics; Plato gave a detailed set of orbital proportions of the planets of our solar system more than a thousand years before the invention of the telescope. Similar ideas and cosmic patterns are found in myth and legend worldwide, but are too often trivialized by the arrogant assumptions of modernist analysts or researchers.

An interesting example is the remarkable book *Hamlet's Mill* by G. DeSantillana and H. VonDechend, wherein the scholars amply demonstrate that myth is a way of describing the cosmos and the solar system, a way that was highly developed in non-literate cultures. But throughout the book, the authors seem to be woefully ignorant of the perennial esoteric traditions of their own (European) culture, and so spend much of their time and text re-inventing wheels, when highly effective vehicles surround them.

The Faery Tradition and Cosmic Wisdom

Let us think of the mythic aspects of the Faery and UnderWorld traditions as our inheritance of cosmic wisdom, rather than as crude attempts to explain phenomena to ignorant and fearful minds. With the help of this resource of ancestral wisdom, we will come into a healing relationship between humanity, the planet, and the other orders of life. We do this by truly understanding that we are a part of the Earth, the Solar System, and the Cosmos.

Until humans remember that the Earth is a vast living being, and that we are a part of that Entity, no amount of intellectual strategies for healing the environment will be truly effective. The Faery and UnderWorld traditions, and their equivalents worldwide, make it clear and unambiguous that humanity is not alone – it is not superior. The Faery tradition, at one of its deeper initiatory levels, teaches that a human is incomplete, and that a complete being is a harmonious fusion of human, Faery, and living creature: the Threefold Alliance.

It is humanity's artificially contrived sense of isolation and antagonism, the lonely child lashing out at the world around it, which has caused our ills. Environmental ills are reflected into human ills, until we truly understand that we are one with the land, the oceans, and the planet.

Once we truly know that we are not unique, but are part of the living world, we can begin the true process of Earth Healing.

The Threefold Alliance

The old tradition teaches that a human being alone is incomplete. Far from being superior, dominant entities created to triumph over and ultimately, it would seem, destroy the Earth, humans have lost the knowledge of their true nature. This loss is what leads to the sense of loneliness and incompleteness that every human feels; and its negative aspects lead to the hostility towards all other living creatures, to the very lands and oceans that give humans their sustenance, and to the planet whereof they have their life.

Humans seek to assuage their loneliness with sexual passion, drugs, trivial machine-centered entertainments that spiral into degrading fantasy and violence. Like angry children, they lash out in rage and rejection from some seemingly petty hurt, but have no real sense of why they strike, even at those who love them, in this case, unseen. Their pain is from their loss. In the Faery tradition we say that they have lost the petals of the rose. The Red Rose of Five Petals is the result of Completion of the Threefold Alliance of Human, Faery, and Living Creature. After Completion with the Fivefold Red Rose, comes Transformation with the Fivefold White Rose, and then the Tenfold Rose brings Emergence. Completion, Transformation of that which was completed, and Emergence into a Renewed World.

To come into the Threefold Alliance, you must go to the Crossroads where the Four Hidden Ways come together; the Four Hidden Ways of the World that make long travels short and short ones heavy with unimagined time.

At the Crossroads, at the place where all orders of life meet together, seek out your Faery allies and companion creatures. You cannot compel them or invoke them, any more than you can compel or invoke human companions in the outer and surfacing world. If you go to the Crossroads with an established idea of the allies that you think you need, you will fail. Those that come and go are those that come and go. They are those that are needful, harmonious, and appropriate.

At first, a host of many will come. But out of that trooping host, some twos or threes will draw close, all together. And from them will come one especially strong for each of the two orders of life, Faery and creature. To one side comes the Faery ally, either to your right or left. To the other side comes the living creature, be it of land, sea, or air. Sense, see, and feel them to your right and to your left. Be still and calm in their company: all three of you strengthen and support one another at the Crossroads.

After communion with them, you may return to your outer world, stepping back from the Crossroads in peace.

Do this over and over, until you are at ease with it.

THE WINGED CROWN

There are many ways to come deeper into the Alliance, and to find the lost petals of the Red Rose. Here is one long taught in the old tradition:

Go to the Crossroads, and come into your Threefold Alliance. Be still, breathing steadily, and wait until they draw close to your right and left.

Place the balls of your thumbs over your eyes, into the eye sockets so that all is dark. The edges of your hands will touch along the midline of your nose and brow. Let your finger fall and wrap flat on your brow, thumbs to your temple, and fingertips to your hair line.

To one side, open the way for your Faery ally, who will merge with you somewhat on that side. On the other side open the way for a spiritual creature, be it of land, sea, or air, which will merge with you somewhat on that side.

Now extend you fingers and thumb straight up and out, stretching them to make a crown. The fingers will radiate upwards and the thumbs out to the sides. This is the Winged Crown.

Now you will feel your companions come closer in to merge with you, through your thumbs. Your right side is of the nature of one, your left is of the nature of the other.

Slowly lift away one hand, and open that eye. You will see as your companion of that side sees. Now slowly lift away the other hand, and open that eye to see as the companion of that side sees. Thus, one eye sees with the Faery sight, and the other sees with the creature sight. This may cause some shaking or vertigo, at first.

After some moments, return the hands one by one to the Winged Crown. Then relax the Winged Crown with fingers wrapped on the skull again.

Now you take down one hand to see again with your human eye, then the other hand to see again with your human eye.

When you are practiced in this art, do it with eyes open while walking about. You will discover that the world is very different from the way you thought it was – from the way you have been falsely taught.

WORKING WITH INNER CONTACTS IN FAERY HEALING

In this chapter we will describe the step by step basic stages of how we work with Faery Healing. These apply no matter what may be your Aptitudes (finding Aptitudes is described in Chapter 3).

The Red Rose of Five Petals

1. Go to the Crossroads, and open out your Threefold Alliance. (The Threefold Alliance is described in this chapter). Do this before doing anything else. It is the first step in all Faery magic, and also the last and most advanced, no matter how many other methods you learn.

2. Go to the Crossroads (or while at the Crossroads), and attune to those allies, Cousins, and Co-Walkers of the Faery realm that will work with you in the tasks of healing.

3. Attune to the healing forces shared and exchanged between yourself and your allies. Let these forces/energies/contacts flow through you, triggering your Aptitude.

4. Work with your allies and your Aptitude(s) in the healing task.

5. Close by going to the Crossroads again. Give thanks and acknowledgement to those spiritual beings that have worked with you.

This fivefold pattern is the basic one for all Faery Healing, regardless of the task or the Aptitudes. There will be times and tasks when you want to open out to other levels. These are described next, and you will find support material for them in various chapters in this book, and also in *Earth Light* and *Power Within the Land*, the earlier companion volumes in this series.

In the Mystery of the Double Rose, each of these stages relates to one of the five petals of the Red Rose, which works through blood. The spiritual and transformative forces can, and do, flow into the human body, according to certain Aptitudes. The Aptitudes are "in the blood," as are some of the allies which are, in tradition, said to be present with certain bloodlines or families. This type of healing is the one referred to in the traditions of the Seventh Child or, in folk tales, the seventh son of a seventh son (but it refers equally to male or female).

The Red Rose healing must flow through the human body before it works through other vehicles. It flows in combination from Faery allies, living creatures, and Ancestors, into and through the human healer.

Remember that the Red Rose is nourished by the River of Tears, shed by the Red Dragon. Likewise the White Rose, to which we will proceed next, is nourished by the River of Blood which is shed by the White Dragon.

The White Rose of Five Petals

The next fivefold pattern relates to the White Rose. In this, we work with forces that do not flow through the human body until the Double Rose is created. These are some of the deeper forces of the Faery Realm and UnderWorld.

1. Go to the Cross roads and open the Well of Light (Chapter 1).
2. Open the way for one or more Go-Betweens (Chapter 2).
3. The Go-Betweens mediate the presence of a Mentor, or Great One from the Faery tradition who rises out of the Well of Light.
4. A union is created whereby spiritual forces flow a) from the Shining Ones deep in the Well of Light; b) to and through the Mentor; c) to and through the Go-Betweens; d) to and through the allies and co-walkers; and then e) outward through the humans. These stages relate to the petals of the White Rose.
5. The connection is then returned, in reverse order, with thanks and acknowledgements, working stage by stage back to the Crossroads as follows: humans, Threefold Alliance, Go-Betweens, Mentor, and Well of Light. We then close our awareness of the Crossroads and the Four Hidden Ways.

The White Rose Healing does not flow directly through the human body, but through the Red Rose Healing. The deeper forces have to be mediated and transformed before they flow out into the outer or surface world.

There is also a specific art of mediating White Rose healing through inner vision, whereby there is no touch or other Aptitude at work physically. Methods of this sort, unfortunately, are widely trivialized in New Age healing, so we must be very clear indeed that we do not confuse or compare the White Rose methods and forces with those of popularized distance healing.

THE MYSTERY OF THE DOUBLE ROSE

Teaching from Inner Contacts

From time to time in my books, published over the last 18 years and more, I have found it helpful to include some material that comes directly from the inner contacts. I must say, immediately, that the inner contacts do not quote or dictate text, and there is no verbatim transcription. Most of the time, I sense input from my inner contacts and I translate this out in workable text for the contemporary reader. They do not offer it as text, but in a completely different way that I will describe shortly. So when you are reading a teaching or communication from inner contacts, such as those I have quoted over the years in various books, you are getting a version that is more direct, less edited, and has a distinct voice that is not my own.

How does it work?

Usually, I attune to the subject matter and receive inner intimations about it. To do this I have to be still and calm, and "feel" my way into the subject. Sometimes, these intimations come very strongly of their own volition, as was the case with the Mystery of the Double Rose. The communication comes without words, but in streams of concepts that are at the very edge of verbal definition. Usually there are no images, but a formless direct transmission. This will come out, through the human mind, as very concentrated, multi-level phrases and sentences. The tone is often archaic, but not in false ancient English. It is archaic because all inner contacts draw some of the communicative power from the collective of ancestral consciousness. This pool is used as a reservoir of energy for the streams of communication. So when specific material is put into words, the language is often multi-level in meaning, and seems to be of an older stratum than, say, modern day street English or that of a television presenter. But there are no mysterious words or fake antiquarianisms, as this is living language, not a romantic mood or reproduction.

Often, a set of related concepts will come all at once, like a complex interwoven knot of several distinct strands. It is my task to open this out so that the reader can read what is woven there. More difficult to describe is something else that happens: I sense and feel the actual energies and processes that are being described. Not, undoubtedly, in full, but as a touch or preview mode of consciousness. I receive resonances or access points that lead into the deeper consciousness and the spiritual forces. If I go back over the material, I can recover those subtle feelings to access the experiences themselves. This is the same method that we use in teaching workshops: students remember by the *feeling*, the subtle tone and touch of the inner contact or energy, and not merely by a set of detailed intellectual notes. This recapitulation by feeling, closely akin to our sense of touch, is what the early poets called reverie, a mode of consciousness in which the imagination is enthused with a shared awareness of much that is outside the individual psyche, of other modes of being, and of other beings.

Here, therefore, is some direct teaching concerning the Mystery of the Double Rose.

Here we will share with you the Mystery of the Double Rose, the Red and White, the Two Rivers, the Two Dragons.

This is a mutable Mystery, not rigid, not systematic. It is fluid and changeable, but always within the two-fold pattern of the Double Rose, each rose having five petals. When the roses are separate, they embody the human world and the Faery or spirit world in separation. When they are united, bringing the two worlds together in peace and harmony, they may unite in two different ways.

Two Unions of the Double Rose

The first union is to intertwine in a helix. This mingling of the rose trees involves many flowers, intertwined as red and white alternatively or in patterns when they bloom. This is the form of interaction through the generations, in time, in nature. We would say that the Roses twine together according to the Moon, and Under the Sun, for they reach from Earth upwards towards Moon, to Sun, in their twining.

The second union is the merging of Red and White as one flower, creating a Rose of Ten Petals. This Tenfold Rose grows within one living entity, unbound by time, in the starry world. We would say that this rose grows neither by the light of the Sun nor of the Moon, but by Earth Light and Star Light only.

The Tenfold Rose is created by the fusion of the Threefold Alliance in the Red Rose, and the Shining Ones, Mentors, and Go-Betweens in the White Rose. In each case, Three becomes Five in the petals, and the two Fives become Ten in the Double Rose, which then becomes One.

The Five Petals of the Red Rose, in and about the human, are thus:

1. the Individual Human (yourself)
2. the Feminine (of yourself and ancestors)
3. the Masculine (of yourself and ancestors)
4. the Faery allies, cousins and co-walkers
5. the companion living creatures

Most humans have scattered their Rose petals, and are not connected to more than the first petal, sometimes also to the second by gender, more rarely to the first, second, and third, regardless of gender. The First Task of the Mystery is to gather the petals that are scattered and discover how they may be unified into a whole Red Rose. The Five Petals of the White

Rose, in and about the UnderWorld, are as follows:

1. the Go-Between(s) (transhuman in the UnderWorld)
2. the Mentor(s) or Great Ones
3. the Shining Ones in the Well of Light that weave upwards
4. the Shining Ones in the Well of Light that weave downward
5. the Source of Earth Light, the One Within the Earth

The White River nourishes the Red Rose, and rises from the UnderWorld to the Overworld, then descends again carrying with it the sorrows of the surface world; hence it is called the River of Tears.

The Red River nourishes the White Rose, and descends from the Overworld to the UnderWorld, passing through the blood of all living creatures, re-ascending again to the Stars. Hence it is called the River of Blood. The Mystery of the River of Blood is discovered through your ability to have its Ascension flow intentionally upward through your own blood (whereas it naturally flows downward therein during its descent). You may enable this Ascension through the Mystery of the Double Rose, for in the White Rose communion, the River of Blood, the Red River, will ascend through the White Rose petals and into your body and blood.

The River of Blood flows from the White Dragon, while the River of Tears flows from the Red Dragon. The White Dragon is in the Stars, whereas the Red Dragon is in the Earth. The twining of the two dragons in the heart of the world occurs where the White Dragon arises from the stars or star dreams within the world, and then communes and twines with the Red Dragon.

This concludes our section on the Mystery of the Double Rose.

With us is the Grace of the Shining Ones in the Mystery of Earth Light. Peace to all Signs and Shadows, Radiant Light to all Ways of Darkness, and the Living One of Light, Secret Unknown, Forever.

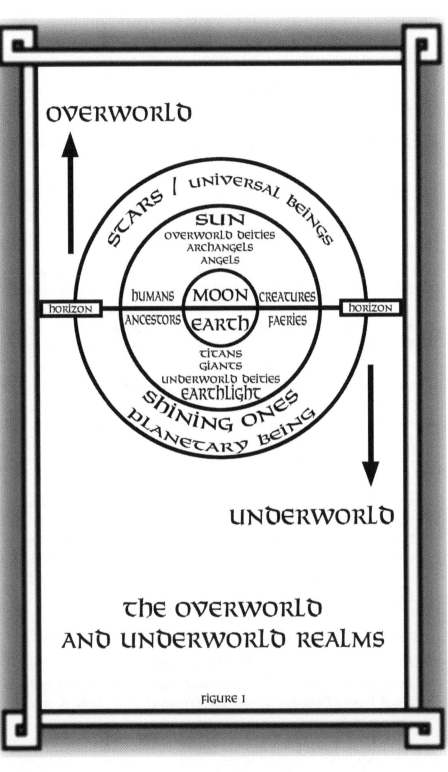

THE OVERWORLD
AND UNDERWORLD REALMS

FIGURE 1

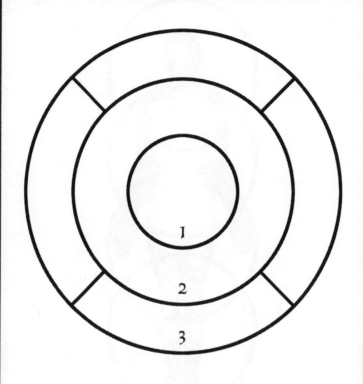

1: SPHERE OF PRIMARY ELEMENT
2: SPHERE OF ACTIVE APTITUDE(S)
3: SPHERE OF FOUR ELEMENTS OVERALL

THE THREE SPHERES OF INTERACTION

FIGURE 2

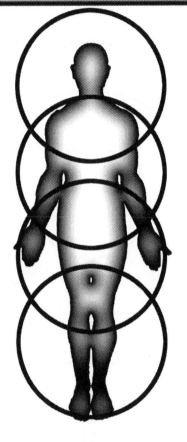

THE ZONES OF THE BODY

1) FEET, LEGS AND THIGH   (EARTH)
2) PELVIS ZONE AND GENITALS (MOON)
3) HEART AND LUNGS   (SUN)
4) THROAT AND HEAD   (STARS)

FIGURE 3

hidden way
of the north

hidden way
of the east

hidden way
of the west

hidden way
of the south

the crossroads

figure 4

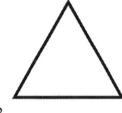

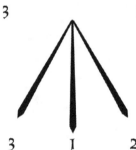

1: ҺUMAN
2: ҒAERY
3: LiⅤiNG CREATURES

ТҺE ТҺREEFOLƉ ALLiANCE

FIGURE 5

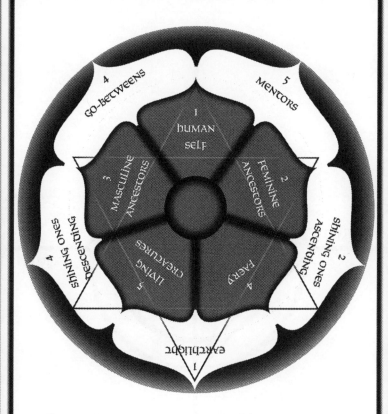

RED ROSE
1: SELF (HUMAN)
2: FEMININE POLARITY/ ANCESTORS
3: MASCULINE POLARITY/ ANCESTORS
4: FAERY
5: LIVING CREATURES

WHITE ROSE
1: EARTHLIGHT
2: SHINING ONES ASCENDING
3: SHINING ONES DESCENDING
4: GO-BETWEENS
5: MENTORS

THE DOUBLE ROSE

FIGURE 6

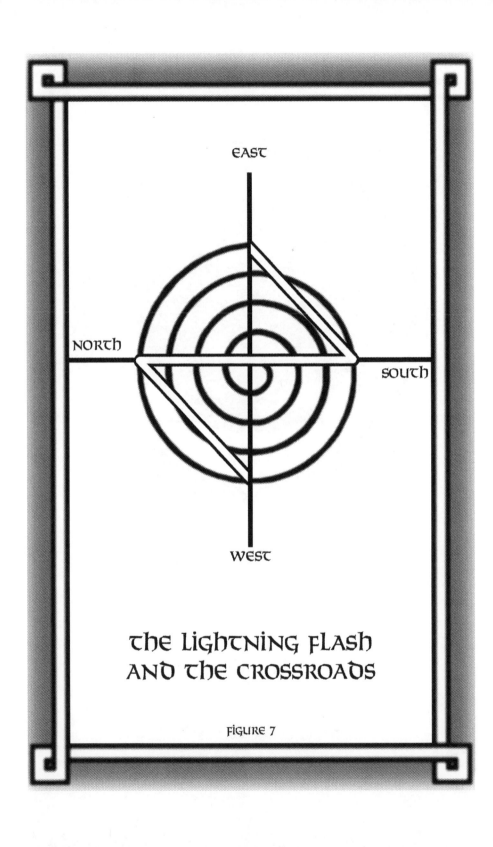

EAST

NORTH

SOUTH

WEST

THE LIGHTNING FLASH
AND THE CROSSROADS

FIGURE 7

Recommended Work Program
for Self Training

Before you read this recommended program, please do not think of "self-training" as some kind of strenuous, lonely effort. You will be working with Faery contacts, cousins, and friends. You will be working with spiritual companion creatures. You will be attuning to the many people that have done, and daily work with, Faery Healing in our classes, workshops, and retreats. You will be attuning to the vast and mightily supportive consciousness of the Ancestors. And you will be attuning to those Go-Betweens and Mentors of our tradition who inspired me to write this book in the first place.

This program is only a recommendation: you do not have to follow it. You can follow your inspirations and intuitions to work with the material in this book. If you do that first, you might later benefit by coming back the recommended work program. Some people prefer, and benefit from, a step-by-step method, and then flying with their inspirations; others prefer the inspiration then the backup learning. Either way will work and you will, with time and practice, of course, have been doing both.

An important note: remember to rest. Days off are good. Magical practices benefit from days off.

1. Read *How to Use This Book,* which is found after the *Introduction*, and follow the basic guidelines therein.
2. Listen to the CD all the way through.

3. Read the book all the way through, like a novel.
4. Begin the following study and experiential program.

The program has nine distinct phases and, in the following example, they are balanced over a nine month period, following lunar months rather than calendar. It is a period of gestation, development, nourishment, and assimilation, as well as one of learning and experience. The nine units could be undertaken in nine weeks, if you prefer, providing you keep to the nine-fold rhythm. You might prefer to start with nine weeks, and then go deeper with the nine-month cycle as a later phase of your training with Faery Healing.

Preliminary Training: Read Chapter 1, *Essential Definitions,* and work with the exercises therein as they come up, section by section. They are usually at the end of each essay, so try them, work with them, and learn them, in the order in which they appear. Even if you have done Faery and UnderWorld work before, I would strongly encourage you to do these simple workings in order, as they set the scene for everything else that will follow. After this initial stage, you will go into a monthly cycle of work. Do not rush; there is plenty of time to do this work. If you choose to follow this program, you will have completed the entire training cycle in less that one year.

Month 1: Working with the CD, go to the Crossroads. Do this form or empowered vision every day at the same time for at least the first week of the first month. Ideally, it should be done for the full month, through the phases of the moon, from full to full. If you cannot do it every day (after the first week of essential daily practice), do it every three days, but do not neglect it. Everything comes from, begins with, and ends with the Crossroads.

This is the main focus of your first month. You may add other forms to your own work cycle after one week of doing the Crossroads form, and you may want to add in those simple forms that you tried during your study of Chapter 1. Remember to rest.

Month 2: Read Chapters 2 and 3, *The Faery Races* and *The Seven Aptitudes*. Work with the forms and training exercises in each chapter and, using the CD, go deeply into the form for finding your

Aptitudes. Stay in this cycle for your second month. Be sure to do some of the work outdoors once you are more familiar with it. Do not take a Walkman or similar item to use the CD outdoors! Do as much as possible from memory, as this will greatly enhance the results, the subtle forces, and the communion with Faery contacts. Do not forget to rest.

Month 3: Read Chapter 4, *Deeper into the Aptitudes.* Do the exercises and forms therein. Remember to go to the Crossroads often. Use this month to repeat, confirm, and solidify everything that you have done so far. Do not go into the later parts of the book at this stage, for it is about consolidation. Remember to rest.

Month 4: Read Chapters 5 and 6, *Offerings* and *Forms and Visions.* While you are reading these chapters (which are very different from one another) do no inner work at all, take a complete break. Chapter 5 will give you food for thought, and Chapter 6 is full of detailed workings, forms, and visions. Just absorb and receive.

Month 4 (continued): Chapter 6, working with the CD, and the text of *The Well of Roses*: spend the rest of the month on this initiatory vision and inner communion. To supplement this, you can work with a recording of *Tam Lin* from my CD *Ballad Magic*, and you will find a text for *Tam Lin* in Appendix One. Meditate upon the connections between the Well of Roses, the Three Heads that rise out of the Well, and the balled of *Tam Lin*.

Month 5: Chapter 6, working with the CD, and the text of *The Hawthorn Road*: spend the month on communion with the Go-Between. You can supplement this with material from *The Living World of Faery* that includes 18th Century descriptions of the wise woman that is in our empowered vision. In Appendix 2 you will find a magical song about the Hawthorn Road, and this is recorded on *More Magical Songs*.

During your work with the Hawthorn Road, include some workings at the Crossroads, and with your Aptitudes. They will begin to change and deepen at this stage. Remember to rest. Watch less or no television.

Month 6: In this pivotal sixth month, we come into the deeper and transcendent Mysteries associated with Earth Healing. Devote the main work of month 6 to *The Oak Mystery* from Chapter 6, and try to work with this once per day. Keep a dream journal in addition to any meditational notes, but do not get bogged down in note-taking. If note-taking starts to dominate, ritually burn all your notes (physically) while at the Crossroads (magically): you will be surprised at how empowering this simple ritual will be! In addition, stay with the Crossroads and the Aptitudes. They will change again, especially the Aptitudes, after you have entered the Oak Mystery.

Month 7: Chapter 6, *The Sacred Mountain* is a form that integrates the human, Faery, and living creature consciousness at a very deep level. Work with this steadily through the month, stage by stage, until you can enter into all three stages from memory. During this month, focus only on the Sacred Mountain. Take several days off any time you wish, but be sure to do this form at least seven times during the month.

Month 8: Chapter 6, *Bridge Building* is a form that is best done by a group of people, but you can work with it along with your Allies, Companions, and Co-Walkers. By now, you are well on the way to having an established Working Team of inner contacts. Use this Bridge Building form cautiously, and do not overdo it – three times in the month will be enough. During this phase, go back over the initial training exercises from Chapter 1, *Essential Definitions*.

Month 9: Chapter 7, *The Mystery of the Double Rose*. Read and study the chapter, and practice the inner forms. This is the most powerful phase of the training course. All your earlier work leads up to this, and prepares you for it.

Copyright and Usage Notice
Please Read Carefully

Due to abuses of copyright after the publication of some of my earlier books, I must make the legal situation clear to all readers and anyone who wishes to work with this book and CD. While I am uncomfortable at having to lay out the rules in this manner, I do so because of the dishonest and unscrupulous actions of a very small number of people, who have all been stopped by legal action.

General Use

You may use this material freely for private and personal use only, or within voluntary group meetings of friends gathering to work with this material. You may not use it, or any part of it, to charge or raise money, to teach classes, to claim to be a healer or practice healing, nor may you include any of it in any courses or publications, in any media known now or in the future. Anyone doing so will be subject to legal action.

Teaching

There are a small number of teachers trained by me to teach this material with permission. If I have not trained you, you cannot use this material for teaching purposes. You cannot be trained by anyone else to teach this material, nor can you receive permission from anyone else, as I am the sole copyright holder. There are no exceptions to this, and attendance at a workshop taught by me, or by one of my approved teachers, does not qualify anyone to teach this material.

Healing

It is absolutely forbidden to use material from this book and CD to claim, advertise, or practice healing for payment, even if you are a qualified healer or therapist with a licensed practice. Faery Healing is not a way of earning a living – it is a Way of Life. Be warned!

Quoting and Fair Usage

All the material in this book and on the accompanying CD is strictly copyright, registered in the US, and protected worldwide by international copyright laws. You may quote *brief* extracts as implied by fair usage in copyright law, and all quotes must be acknowledged or they are illegal. Many brief quotes in one printed or published item are an infringement of copyright, and will result in legal action.

Other than acceptable brief quotes, material from this book or CD may not be reproduced in any way in any medium existing now or in the future, and permission is *not* given for it to appear in any form on the Internet.

Requesting Permissions

Permission must be sought in writing for any use, and copyright infringement is taken seriously and will always be pursued by legal action. Email is an acceptable form for requesting permission, but merely sending an email request (or a letter) does *not* automatically give permission. Only a reply from me will define permission or refusal of permission. You can mail requests to PO Box 5128, Laurel, MD 20726, or you can contact me direct by emailing rjstewart@dreampower.com with any requests to quote from this book for review or educational purposes, or with any other requests regarding the material in the book or on the CD. No honest and reasonable request, within the rules of copyright law, will be turned down.

R.J. Stewart, 2003

Appendix One:
The Initiatory Ballads

There are two primary initiatory ballads for the Scottish Faery tradition: *Tam Lin* and *Thomas Rhymer*. They connect in many ways to the European Faery tradition and to the UnderWorld tradition in general, forming a small part of a body of magical ballads that contain motifs and imagery from a pagan or pre-Christian era. Such magical ballads were known all over Britain in the language or dialect of the ordinary people, and were carried to America by emigrants, bondservants, and slaves. A strong tradition of ballad singing survived in the communities of the southern Appalachian Mountains. To the best of my knowledge, neither of the two Faery initiatory ballads survived in Appalachian or American folk tradition, and all versions found in the United States today are re-creations by enthusiasts, and do not come direct from American oral tradition. This is not surprising, as they are highly specialized ballads with local traditions attached. There are, however, many other magical ballads that survived in American tradition, some long after they had died out of use in Britain and Ireland.

In Scotland, ballads such as *Tam Lin* and *Thomas Rhymer* (and many more) were sung in a dialect that is sometimes called Lallans or lowland Scottish English, not in Gaelic. Scottish English appeared in the lowlands of Scotland at some time in the early middle ages, and was highly developed and used by many superb medieval poets, such as the master William Dunbar. Yet the ballads are from oral folk tradition, and are not the product of known writers; they are in a very simple direct vernacular poetry, such as is found in folk tradition in the various languages of Europe. Many of the vernacular magical ballads known in English are also found in several other languages and countries, so it seems likely that they were circulated by traveling singers and storytellers at an early date. Traditional magical ballads contain mythic themes involving death, resurrection, shape changing, and often have a mysterious female figure that acts as the ultimate arbiter or power in the story. By working with the iconographic method (popularized by Robert Graves), we can explore the images in each verse and discover how they relate to mythic themes, no matter how the song itself rationalizes the action.

The magical ballads of Scotland, Ireland, and Britain, of which there are many and in all dialects, do not preserve a Gaelic tradition. Yet they contain ancient mythic and magical themes, and very specific initiatory magical imagery. At a deeper level, they contain the secrets of initiation into the Faery tradition, or the mysteries of the Goddess.

Many ballads are generally magical, and do not contain detailed initiatory content. *Tam Lin* and *Thomas Rhymer*, however, are extremely detailed. You only need these two ballads to encompass the entire Faery and UnderWorld tradition – if you know how to work with them. There is no doubt in my mind that these two ballads were used as teaching and training devices for the Faery tradition; but there is no historical proof of this theory. Each ballad works in a different way, and a short comparison is enlightening.

- *Tam Lin* features the Faery Queen as a dark and frightening power, while
- *Thomas Rhymer* features her as a light and beneficent power.

- *Tam Lin* is about the ultimate triumph of human love over the powers of the other world.
- *Thomas Rhymer* is about the triumph of understanding of the UnderWorld mysteries.

- *Tam Lin* embodies sexual and blood mysteries of birth, transformation, and rebirth.
- *Thomas Rhymer* embodies the deeper mysteries beyond sexuality and the cycle of death and rebirth.

- *Tam Lin* describes the sensuous communion between human and nature, featuring the rose, the well, fertility magic, and the Crossroads in the surface world as a place of ritual.
- *Thomas Rhymer* describes the spiritual communion between human and Faery featuring the Rivers of Blood and Tears, the Tree of Life, and the Crossroads in the UnderWorld as a place of choice, dedication, and service.

Together, these two ballads offer a relatively complete initiation into the magical consciousness of the Faery realm and UnderWorld. One opens us out to the sexual and sensuous aspects of Faery magic relating to fertility, death, and rebirth; while the other opens us out to the UnderWorld aspects of transpersonal understanding and prophecy. While *Tam Lin* talks of human love, *Thomas Rhymer* talks of service. We need to experience the subtle forces of both, for they mutually empower one another. It would be tempting to rationalize them, and say that *Tam Lin* is phase one and *Thomas Rhymer* phase two, but this is mere reductionism. Each ballad is, ultimately, about *transformative power*, not about artificially graded stages of so-called progress.

My experience, working with these ballads for most of my life, is that we need the spiritual forces raised by both, and that they are active invocations of power more than they are sources of teaching through exposition, drama, and imagery. The teaching is there, of course, and I have explored it in depth in books such as *The UnderWorld Initiation* and in many workshops and classes. But the spiritual and magical power flows whenever the ballads are sung, even if the singer or the listeners have no understanding of the teachings.

You can hear a number of magical ballads, including *Tam Lin* and *Thomas Rhymer*, on my CD *Ballad Magic*. These are sung as invocations, without instruments, and are recorded live with a group of listeners. The psychic and spiritual forces are very different in such a recording to those of a studio piece without listeners, where instruments are dubbed and even single notes re-digitized and edited. In such a context there cannot be magical invocation. I say "listeners," but in the sharing of a live magical ballad, they are really participants in a ritual invocation rather than a passive audience.

Here are the texts of both ballads, with the dialect simplified somewhat for the modern reader. These are the versions that I sing. There are many others with the same basic plot but variations in the verses. There is no complete or authoritative text, as the ballads were preserved in memory and oral tradition. They were only written down by scholars in recent times, so the idea of a "complete" or "full" version, as sometimes proposed, is not only historical nonsense, but it totally misses the subtle truth of magical ballads in a diffuse protean oral tradition. They survived because they were incomplete and unnoticed, because they lived in the magical awareness of ordinary people. We owe much to those ancestors who kept such songs and stories alive.

TAM LIN

The King forbad his maidens a'
  that wore gold in their hair,
  tae come or go by Carterhaugh
  for the young Tam Lin is there.

And those that go by Carterhaugh
  from them he tak's a fee
  either their rings or their mantels
  or else their maidenheed.

So Janet has kilted her green mantel
  just a little above her knee
  and she has gane tae Carterhaugh
  just as fast as she cud flee

And when she come tae Carthaugh
   Tam Lin was at the well
   that is his horse was there
   but awa' was himsel'

She hadnae pu'ed a double rose
   a rose but three or fair
   when up and spoke the young Tam Lin
   cried "Lady pu' nae mair!"

"How dare ye pu' those flo'ors
   how dare ye break those wands
   how dare ye cam tae Carterhaugh
   withouten my command?"

She says "Carterhaugh it is my ain
   my daddy gave it t'me
   and I will cam and gae by here
   withouten any leave of thee!"

There were four and twenty ladies gay
   all sitting doon at chess
   and in an' cam the fairy young Janet
   as green as any glass.

Up an' spake her faither dear
   he spake up meek an' mild
   "Oh alas Janet" he cried
   " I fear you go with child"

"And if I go with child
   indeed it is myself tae blame
   there's not a laird in a' your hall!
   Sall give my child his name!"

And Janet has kilted her green mantle
   just a little above her knee
   and she has gain tae Carterhaugh
   for tae pu' the scathing tree.

"How dare ye pu' those flo'ors
  all amang the leaves sae green
  an' ye wud kill that bonnie babe
  that we gat us between"

She says "Ye must tell tae me Tam Lin
  ah ye must tell tae me
  were ye e'er a mortal knight
  or mortal hall did see?"

"I was onc't a mortal knight
  I cam riding here one day
  and I fell fram aff my horse
  the Faery queen stole me awa"

"Tomorrow night is Hallowe'en
  and the Faery folk do ride
  those that wud their true love win
  at Miles Cross they must hide"

"First ye let pass the black horse
  then ye let pass the broun
  run ap tae the milk white steed
  and pu' the rider doon"

" I Tam a Lin on an milk white steed
  Wi' a gold star in my croon
  because I was a mortal knight
  they give me such renknown"

"First they'll change me in your airms
  intae some snake or adder
  hold me close and fear me not
  for I'm yair child's fadder"

"Next they'll change me in your airms
  intae a lion wild
  hold me close and fear me not
  just as yu'ld hold your child"

"Then they'll change me in your airms
into a burning gleed
throw me into well water
and through me in with speed"

" Last they'll change me in your airms
into a mother-naked knight
wrap me up in your green mantel
and hide me close from sight"

So weel she did what he did say
she did her tru' love win
and wrapt him up in her manter
as blithe any bird in Spring.

Up and spake the Faery Queen
from oot a bush o' broom
"Oh alas my sisters a'
Young Tam Lin has escaped his doom"

Up and spake the Faery Queen
and angry cried she
"If I had known of this Tam Lin
that some lady'd borrowed thee...

If had known of this Tam Lin
that some lady'd borrowed thee
I'd plucked out thine eyes of flesh
And put in eyes of a tree...

If I had known of this Tam Lin
before we cam frae home
I'd plucked out thin heart of flash
and put in a heart of stone"

In some versions, Tam Lin is described as a potential human sacrifice to the "powers of Hell." As this seems to be propaganda, I do not sing these verses, even though I respect and understand that this propagandist element has helped the ballad to survive through centuries of Christianity.

My understanding is that the deeper, more hidden implication is that Tam Lin had become the lover of the Faery Queen, and was slowly losing his humanity. This is a teaching that is found in many forms in Faery tradition, about the charm and power of Faery lovers, and losing one's humanity. In *Thomas Rhymer*, however, the man attempts to worship the Faery Queen as the Queen of Heaven, and she educates him with the visions of the UnderWorld.

I had been singing this ballad for many years, and had always thought of the last few verses as retrospective dark curses from the Faery Queen, angry with Tam Lin being rescued from the Faery realm by a human lover. But during an intense Faery workshop, someone pointed out to me that the curses mean something different. They imply that if Tam Lin had remained, losing his human awareness gradually, he would have be able to see as a tree sees, becoming absorbed into tree-consciousness, losing his human perception and not susceptible to the charms of human glamour. Next he would have gone deeper, and would have been able to feel as a stone feels, over vast periods of time and planetary life, and not be dominated by ephemeral human emotion. This is a very interesting way of interpreting the curses that close the ballad, which I think has a lot to offer in meditation and inner contemplation. Nor does it preclude the maledictions of the Faery Queen, who says what she would have done, had she known!

THOMAS RHYMER

Whereas Tam Lin is a character of folklore and tradition, Thomas Rhymer is an historical person. This is, in itself, highly significant: for Thomas was a Scottish poet living in the Lowlands in the 13th Century. Yet his name and story passed deeply into Scottish tradition and folklore; so much so, that he is found in Gaelic Faery lore and in traditional stories and practices centuries after his death. So what is it about Thomas that caused his name to be so widely associated with the Faery tradition in Scotland? In short, he is a

Go-Between: a transhuman living in the Faery realm. This is how the Scots have understood him for centuries, though the modern terminology is my own. If a farmer had trouble with a herd or piece of sour land, he would seek a dream of Thomas Rhymer to help mediate with the Faeries of the land, drawing upon the tradition that the Faeries could heal and change if the right person solicited them in the right way. If a poet sought inspiration, he would think of Thomas as his model, tapping into the enduring tradition of poetry and music shared between humans and Faeries. More significantly for us today, if a Faery seer, seeress, or healer sought to travel deeply into the Faery realm and UnderWorld, it was Thomas that was often sought as a guide – for he is the classic Go-Between, Guide, Prophet, and Poet of the Faery tradition.

The vernacular ballad of *Thomas Rhymer* must date from some time after the 13th Century, as the story is associated with Thomas Earlston who lived in the Eildon district at that time. He was author of several long poems that have survived, and there is a literary version of same story told in the ballad, but as a long verse narrative. Thomas may not be the author of this version, but it is often associated with him as it tells his story. It is more likely that a medieval Scottish poet took a powerful tale already in circulation and made a literary version of it sometime after Thomas' death. There is also a set of vernacular prophecies associated with Thomas, and editions bearing his name were printed as popular almanacs as late as the 19th Century.

The folk ballad, however, was circulated and preserved among the ordinary country people, and it is to this source that we should attribute some of the folkloric beliefs, in addition to stories and practices associated with Thomas as a Go-between, an intermediary for humans in the Faery realm, and a willing spokesman for any who seek out Faery contact.

Whereas Tam Lin died out as a traditional ballad, at least until the popular folk revival of the 1960s, after which it had many resurrections (though not as a true traditional song), there is some evidence that country people continued to sing versions of *Thomas Rhymer*, especially Scottish gypsies. As a broad rule, it seems that gypsies in Britain and Ireland preserved old traditions of music and song after they were all but extinct among the rest of the population.

Thomas Rhymer is the most detailed initiatory ballad that we have, bar none. It tells the story of a historical poet associated with the Faery tradition, and of how he went, physically, into the hollow hills with the Queen of Elfland. There he was shown the visions and powers of the UnderWorld: the Rivers of Tears and Blood, the Tree of Life, and the Crossroads Beneath. These components come from a specific Mystery, which brings prophecy, poetry, and communion within the Faery realm. Hence, the long folkloric association of Thomas and the Faeries in Scottish tradition.

Thomas Rhymer

True Thomas lay on grassy bank
and he beheld a lady gay
a lady that was brisk and bold
to come riding o'er the ferny brae.

Her skirt was of the grass-green silk
her mantle of the velvet fine
and on every lock of her horse's mane
hung fifty siller bells and nine.

True Thomas he took of his hat
and bowed him low down to his knee
"All hail thou Virgin Queen of Heaven
for thy like on Earth I ne'er did see".

"Oh no, oh no, true Thomas" she cried
"that name does not belong to me,
for I am the queen of faire Elfland
that's come for tae visit here with thee."

And Thomas ye maun gae wi' me
True Thomas ye maun gae wi' me
An' you maun serve me seven long years

thro' weal or woe as may chance to be".
She's mounted on the milk white steed
and took true Thomas up ahind
and aye whene'er the bridel rang
the steed flew faster than the wind.

For forty days and forty nights
they wad thro' red blude to the knee
and they saw neither sun nor moon
but heard the roaring of the sea.

For forty days and forty nights
they wade thro' red blude to the knee
for all the blood that's shed here above
lights down thro' the streams of that countrie.

The saw neither sun nor moon
but heard the roaring of the sea
for all the tears that's shed here above
light down thro' the streams of that countrie.

They rade on and further on
'til they came unto a tree:
"Oh light ye doon ye lady faire
and I'll pull o' that fruit for thee".

"Oh no, oh no, true Thomas" she said
"that fruit may not be pu'd by thee
for all the plagues of the world above
light down on the fruit of this countrie"

"But I have bread here in my lap
likewise a bottle of red wine
and ere that we go further on
ye sall rest, and ye sall dine."

When he'd eaten and dranken his fill
she said "lay your head doon on my knee,
and ere we climb yon high high hill
I'll show ye wonders three...

See ye not that narrow narrow way
beset with thorns and briars?
That is the path of righteousness
Tho after it few inquires.

See ye not that broad broad way
that winds aboot the lilly leven?
That is the path of rank wickedness
tho some teach you it is the road tae he'en.

And see ye not the bonny bonny way
that winds aboot the ferny brae?
Oh that is the path tae fair Elfland
where ye and I maun gae.

True Thomas ye must hold your tongue
whate'er ye chance tae hear or see
and ye will serve me seven long yeer
thro' weel or woe as may chance tae be. "

And he has gotten a coat of woven cloth
likewise the shoes of velvet green
Until seven years were past and gone
True Thomas ne'er on earth was seen.

Note: when I explored the inner meaning of this ballad in *The UnderWorld Initiation* some years ago, I understood the Crossroads to be that of three choices: righteousness, wickedness, and Faery. The fourth road, of course, is the one down which Thomas and the Queen of Elfland have traveled from the human realm above. That interpretation still holds good, but there are some further connections to the Threefold Alliance that may be added here.

The narrow road of righteousness, beset with thorns and briars, is the way of righteousness for humanity. It is also the path of the Living Creatures, who (in medieval conception) are without Original Sin. The creatures, as in many folk tales, can pass unscathed through the briars, while the humans may not until they have passed some tests of intention (righteousness). The road of wickedness, winding pleasantly among the lilies, is the road of sensuous distraction with an added satire against Christianity. This is the road of ancestral mistakes, the lure of temporal wealth and power, again with a typical medieval tone alluding to the wealth of the Church. So this is the human road in the UnderWorld, wherein the power may be sought for the wrong reasons. And the Faery road winds around the ferny brae, or slope, leading to the inner palaces of the Faery realm. So the three roads relate to Innocence/Righteousness/ Creatures, Wickedness/Illusion/Humanity, and Balance/Nature/ Faery.

WORKING WITH THE BALLADS

There is much more to both of these ballads, of course, and they will give a lifetime of Faery insights if you choose to work with them. Remember that it is the power that is important, more so than a textual interpretation. I would encourage you to learn one of the traditional melodies, and sing these ballads while communing in the Threefold Alliance. The singing aloud enhances the power considerably, and it does not have to be an artistic performance.

As you sing, build the images of each verse strongly in your inner vision. You will feel the power come through, and you will feel levels that are not accessible in words. If you feel unsure about singing, work with the recordings of empowered singing that I have made, or any other recording that appeals to you.

Appendix Two:
Initiatory Songs

The songs that follow are all original magical songs, coming from Inner Contact over a number of years. I have recorded them on various albums, and some are connected to stories in my anthology *Magical Tales*; though in all such connections, the songs came first and the stories unfolded out the songs.

Each of these songs has a vision and some ritual or ceremonial act connected to it, which is briefly described. They are intended for you to sing, recite, and share. They can be found, along with other magical songs, on *More Magical Songs*. (Recordings and books can be found at www.rjstewart.net if you cannot obtain them from your local bookstore.)

Please note: if you record these songs or perform them, you must follow the laws of copyright in all cases. You may not record publish or distribute these songs without formal permission. For permissions, please contact me at rjstewart@dreampower.com, and no reasonable request will be turned down.

THE OAK SONG

This song is associated with the Mystery of the Priest King and Priestesses Queens, the Oak Tree Mystery.

Chorus:

And if you knew the same as I
You'ld do as I have done
And raise your life unto the sky
And root in the earth and stones.

When I was nothing, nothing was I,
All locked in the fruit on the tree
That raised me up to the summery sky
Then down on the ground to lie.

Through the years I rooted and I grew
And many men sought out my way,
Under my branches kings they slew
In the moon and the sun marked days.

I fall not neither do I fail
My seed is like the rain
That scatters far upon the ground
And flourishes forth again.

THE HAWTHORN ROAD

The Hawthorn Road is a very fine road
From where you stand to over the hill
But the stones are hard and the way is long
And you won't go far if you just stand still,
you won't go far if you just stand still
on the Hawthorn Road.

The Hawthorn Road is dark and old
It waits where the other roads never run
There's no signposts or wayside inns
And it's all starlit, without Moon or Sun,
all starlit without Moon or Sun
on the Hawthorn Road.

The Hawthorn road has no milestones
  But each beat of your heart as it pumps your blood,
  Where I have been, there you may go,
  For the Hawthorn Road survives the flood,
  the Hawthorn Road survives the flood
  on the Hawthorn Road.

THE WEAVERS SONG AND CEREMONY

The Weaver's Song is a Crossroads song to be sung, ideally, while standing at the Crossroads. It came to me originally as a vision of an ancestor dying at the center of the Directions, in a stone circle. His death was a peaceful, beautiful event. In the vision, I heard, but did not see, women singing a song that took the spirit out to the Crossroads, and also brought a spirit back into birth for the next turning of the Wheel. Their song also held the secret of liberation from the turning of the Wheel. It is all in this song and, like some aspects of the ballad of *Tam Lin*, this is also a song about human love and lovemaking, so it works at several levels at once. After the song itself, you will find the ritual that goes with the song. This is a Crossroad ritual for a group of people, though one person can also do it as a solo ceremony if necessary.

The Weaver Song

Now for you I weave some weaving
  Listen to it well,
  Now for you I twist some twining
  Listen to its spell:

Once I was held in the eyes of the night
  Once in the voice of the day
  Once in the arms of a child all alone
  And once in the mind of a stone.
  In and in the words are weaving
  Through these eyes so blind

Through and through your own heart's listening
Be your soul entwined.

Once I gained a seed from the dawn
Once the jewel from a nest,
Once the light from a fair lady's mirror,
And once a word from the West.

Now it is ending slow your breathing
Now your joys are mine,
Through and through you hold my weaving
In your own design

Gone are the places of whispering stones
Open the gates of the star ways,
Still are the voices that echoed alone
But Peace is a secret unknown.

The Weaver Ceremony

This ceremony was first published in the book *Paths to Peace*, a collection of prayers, ceremonies, and chants from many traditions (ed: John Matthews, Rider, London, 1992). It has been done by many people over the years, and is offered here for your use as a Crossroads ceremony for Faery Healing, Earth Healing, and Peace.

This may be conducted by any number of people, each being allocated roles around the circle. People stand as follows:

- East
- South
- West
- North
- The Opener of Gates: Northeast and Center
- Further people are aligned according to each Direction if necessary

The Directions, the circle dance and the 'Z' pattern.

1. All: The ceremony begins in silence, each of the Four Directions holding a candle. All turn their attention inwards towards peace.

2. Opener: Peace is a secret unknown.
    All: Still are the voices that echoed alone.
    Opener: Open the Gates of the Star-ways.
        (Lights candle or flame in center)
    All: Gone are the places of whispering stones.

3. Opener: From one thread of light are all words and all worlds woven and no single part is severed from the whole. Let us summon the power of the Weaver here among us, according to the pattern of the mystery. (Takes taper, lights it from central flame and then passes it to East)

4. East: (Lights Eastern flame with taper)
    I call upon the power of the East to awaken and attend through this blessed Gate:
        By the power of Air,
        By the power of Dawn,
        By the power of Life.
            (Hands taper to South, who lights Southern flame)

5. South: I call upon the power of the South to arise and attend through this blessed Gate:
        By the power of Fire,
        By the power of bright Noonday,
        By the power of Light.
            (Hands taper to West, who lights Western flame)

6. West: I call upon the power of the West to increase and attend through this blessed Gate:
        By the power of Water,
        By the power of Sunset,

By the power of Love.
    (Hands taper to North, who lights Northern flame)

7. North: I call upon the power of the North to appear and attend through this blessed Gate:
    In the name of the power of Earth,
    By the power of the Mirror of Stars,
    By the power of Law and Liberty.

8. All: resonate HUM, AUM or AMEN, according to choice, and focus attention upon the central light.

9. East: Now for you I weave some weaving;
    Listen to it well.
    Now for you I twist some twining
    Listen to its spell:

10. All: Once I was held in the eyes of the night,
      (Arms raised in the sign of Stars)
    Once in the voice of the Day,
      (Arms held out level in the sign of the Sun)
    Once in the arms of a child alone,
      (Arms crossed in the sign of Humanity)
    And once in the mind of a stone.
      (Arms held downwards in the sign of the Earth)

11. East: In and in the words are weaving
    Through these eyes so blind;
    Through and through you hold my weaving
    In your own design.
      (Pauses before proceeding)

12. East: Once I gained a seed from the Dawn,
    South: Once the jewel from a nest,
    North: Once the light from a fair lady's mirror,
    West: Once a word from the West.

13. West: Now it is ending,
    Slow your breathing,
    Now your joys are mine
    Through and through you hold my weaving
    In your own design.

14. All: Gone are the places of whispering stones,
    Open the Gates of the Star-ways,
    Still are the voices that echoed alone,
    Peace is a secret unknown.

15. Opener: The Opener chants AMEN; all chant AMEN
    (or resonate HUM Or AUM).

16. East Begins: A circle dance begins, led by East (if space permits). All except the Opener move East/South/West/North, awakening to the energies of each Quarter as they pass.

17. Opener: The Opener allows the energies to build as required, then strikes a gong or claps his/her hands three times. East now changes the direction of the dance to pass East/South/North/West three times. After third 'Z' movement, all return sunwise (clockwise) to their original positions.

18. All: All pause here for silent meditation.

19. Opener: The Opener extinguishes the central light, using the Crossing Formula as follows:
    In the name of the Star Father,
    The Earth Mother,
    The True Taker,
    The Great Giver,
    One Being of Light.

20. All: All resonate HUM, AUM or AMEN and depart in silence.

The Stone Chant

This simple chant attunes us to Ancestral presence.

Oh the tall stones standing
where the green grass grows
and the one place of crossing
where the water flows.

(chorus is lilted without words, after each verse)

Raise up the spear
and raise up the horn
and blessed by the place
where our people were born.

All around the circle
sound the voices singing
dance in the sun's path
to set the circle ringing.

Oh the tall stones standing
where the green grass grows
and the one place of crossing
where the water flows.

Lightning Source UK Ltd.
Milton Keynes UK
UKHW04f0109170718
325817UK00001B/93/P